Smart Financial Decision

Mastering Borrowell's Platform for Credit Monitoring and Identity Protection

By

Richardson Rolls

Richardson Rolls, Copyright © 2024.

All rights reserved.

Remember, you must obtain permission from the publisher before duplicating or reproducing this content in any way. As such, neither electronic storage nor transfer nor retention in a database are possible for the content. The publisher or creator must consent before any document part may be copied, scanned, faxed, or kept on file.

Table of Contents

Chapter One: A Unique Approach to Financial Health with Borrowell 1
    Background of the Company 8
    Goals and objectives 17
Chapter Two: Free Credit Report and Score 30
    Comprehending Your Credit Report 40
    The advantages of weekly updates 51
Chapter Three: Making a Personal Loan Application 59
    Loan Term and Interest Rates 71
    Use Cases: Home renovations, debt consolidation, and more 82
Chapter Four: Monitoring Credit: Configuring credit surveillance 101
    Notifications and Alerts for Credit Monitoring 111
    Protection Against Theft of Identity 123
Chapter 5: Suggestions for Financial Products 134
    Customized Credit Card Product Recommendations 138
    Personalized Mortgage Product Recommendations 142
    Personalized Insurance Product Recommendations 145
Chapter 6: An AI-Powered Financial Advisor, Meet Molly 150
    How Molly Examines Your Bank Information 156
Chapter 7: Success Stories and Testimonials from Users 163
    How Borrowell Contributed to Better Financial Well-Being 168
Chapter 8: Use QR Codes and Links 173
    Referral Program Advantages 179
Chapter 9: Opening to Borrowell Registration 184
    Summary of Credit Score 188
About the Author 198

Chapter One: A Unique Approach to Financial Health with Borrowell

Borrowell, a leading fintech enterprise in Toronto, Canada, aims to empower individuals with the knowledge and resources they need to manage their finances effectively. The company's individualized financial solutions, which blend technology, data, and human understanding, cater to various needs.

The Origin of Borrowell

Co-founders Andrew Graham and Eva Wong identified a need among many Canadians for assistance in understanding and managing their credit. In response, they developed a platform that simplifies credit management and offers practical advice for improving one's financial situation. Their goal was to make financial tools easily accessible, understandable, and applicable to help people make smarter financial decisions.

Principal providers and services

Free Credit Report and Score

One of Borrowell's signature offerings is the provision of free credit reports and score access. This tool empowers users by providing them with information on their credit health and is accessible to any Canadian with an internet connection. To provide this service, Borrowell has a partnership with Equifax, one of the biggest credit bureaus. Consumers can track improvements in their credit scores and pinpoint areas for development by receiving weekly updates.

Users can better understand the variables influencing their credit score by consulting the credit report, which provides comprehensive details about credit accounts, payment histories, and inquiries. By providing this service without charge, Borrowell lowers a significant obstacle to financial literacy and equips customers with the means to begin managing their finances.

Individual Loans

Borrowell offers personal loans to assist borrowers in managing their debt, funding major expenditures, or paying for unforeseen bills. The application process is simple and expedient, using technology to allow for a prompt assessment of creditworthiness and the provision of attractive interest rates. Medical costs, home renovations, and debt reduction are just a few uses for Borrowell loans.

Borrowell wants to make borrowing less scary and more approachable by offering a clear and quick loan process. The company's strategy differs from traditional lenders because it emphasizes the customer experience and uses data to provide individualized loan choices.

Credit Surveillance

Borrowell provides credit monitoring in addition to its credit score and report service. With this service, users can receive real-time warnings about any changes to their credit report, including inquiries, new accounts, and possible indications of identity theft. Credit monitoring is essential to keeping your credit in good standing and guarding against fraud.

The user-friendly Borrowell credit monitoring service sends notifications via email or the Borrowell app. This proactive strategy aids users in staying informed and acting promptly in the event of an unforeseen circumstance.

Investment product suggestions

Another feature of Borrowell's platform is personalized recommendations for financial products. By examining consumers' credit profiles and economic habits, Borrowell recommends solutions that can assist them in reaching their financial objectives. Better credit cards, mortgages with lower interest rates, and insurance plans with greater coverage are a few examples.

With these recommendations, customers may be sure they receive the most significant selections because they are transparent and objective. Borrowell's mission is to help consumers save money and choose wisely among financial products.

Molly, the AI-Powered Financial Coach

Besides its primary services, Borrowell provides Molly, an AI-driven financial advisor. Based on customers' financial data, Molly offers tailored advice and insights that help people manage debt, raise their credit score, and save money. Because Molly customizes her counsel to each user's specific financial circumstances, it is a valuable resource for anyone trying to do better with money.

Molly makes money management less intimidating by using data analytics and machine intelligence to provide practical guidance. By simplifying complicated financial concepts into simple advice, Molly helps consumers make better financial decisions and stick to their financial objectives.

The Effect of Borrowell

Borrowell's creative approach to financial health has dramatically benefited its users. Millions of Canadians have benefited from Borrowell's free credit score and report access, individualized financial guidance, and streamlined loan application processes, all of which have helped them take charge of their economic destiny. In the fintech sector, the company stands out for its dedication to financial literacy, transparency, and user experience.

Creating a Community of Financial Literates

Creating a Community of Financial Literates dedicated to enhancing financial literacy, Borrowell is a community as much as a fintech startup. Borrowell's commitment to arming people with the information necessary to make wise financial decisions is evident in its provision of instructional materials, user support, and a blog. The organization routinely produces articles with helpful advice to assist consumers in navigating their financial journeys, including subjects like budgeting, credit management, and saving.

Partnerships with institutions that support financial literacy are another aspect of Borrowell's community activities. Borrowell aspires to improve financial education in Canada by working with government, non-profit, and educational organizations to reach a wider audience

The prospects for Borrowell

The prospects for Borrowell's innovation and client empowerment are central to Borrowell's future goals as it expands. The business is always looking for new ways to use data and technology to improve its offerings and give customers more value. Possible future advancements include new financial products, enhanced credit monitoring tools, and more instructional resources. This commitment to innovation and improvement promises an exciting future for Borrowell and its users.

Because of its dedication to its users and mission, Borrowell will continue to pioneer the fintech sector and work tirelessly to increase everyone's access to financial health.

Recap

Borrowell's path to becoming a preeminent fintech business is evidence of its dedication to enhancing Canadians' financial well-being. Personalized product suggestions, personal loans, credit monitoring, free credit reports and scores, and an AI-powered financial coach are just a few services Borrowell offers to empower customers to manage their money. The company's dedication to openness, innovation, and financial literacy sets it apart and establishes it as a reliable partner in its consumers' financial journeys. With Borrowell, users can feel confident and in control of their financial decisions.

In the climax, Borrowell is more than just a service provider—it is a driving force for financial empowerment. It provides materials and tools that simplify and increase accessibility to financial management for all.

Background of the Company

The idea of Borrowell's co-founders, Andrew Graham and Eva Wong, is where the narrative starts. They recognized a significant gap in many Canadians' financial lives: a lack of access to credit information and the means to handle it appropriately. The goal of Borrowell's founding in 2014 was to close the gap between the low level of financial literacy and the frightening and inaccessible nature of traditional financial services. The company's founding principles were democratizing access to financial information and providing people with the skills and information they need to make better financial decisions.

Vision and Mission of the Founders

Combining their backgrounds in strategy and finance with Eva Wong's knowledge of operations and business development, the two men were able to construct a fintech company that was approachable, creative, and focused on the needs of its customers. They envisioned a platform that would offer free credit reports and scores, along with products and financial advice specific to the needs of each user. Their goal was to assist individuals in making wise choices around credit, debt, and personal money.

The Early Years: Difficulties and Successes

Early on, Borrowell had to overcome the difficulty of building confidence and trust in a market that conventional financial institutions controlled. In Canada, the idea of providing free credit scores was still relatively new, and many people needed clarification about the usefulness and reliability of this kind of service. However, Borrowell swiftly gained popularity by consistently trying to educate the public and provide a user-friendly platform.

A significant early achievement for Borrowell was establishing a collaboration with Equifax, one of the biggest credit reporting agencies globally. Through this cooperation, Borrowell could offer its users accurate and trustworthy credit reports and ratings, which is essential for establishing credibility and trust. The partnership further demonstrated Borrowell's dedication to truth and openness in its offerings.

Development and Extension: Achieving Millions

With a solid foundation and a clear mission, Borrowell flourished. The company's user base expanded as more Canadians realized the value of having free access to their credit reports and scores. The company's continuous innovation and commitment to meeting the evolving needs of its clients have been key to Borrowell's success. The impact of Borrowell's services can be seen in the improved financial decisions and increased financial literacy among its users.

A Look at Personal Loans

One of Borrowell's major service expansions was the addition of personal loans. Recognizing the need for accessible and reasonably priced credit solutions among a large number of Canadians, Borrowell used technology to streamline the loan application process. This strategic move allowed Borrowell to offer flexible terms and competitive interest rates, providing users with a convenient option to obtain loans. The process of adding personal loans to Borrowell's services involved extensive market research, technological development, and regulatory compliance, showcasing the company's commitment to meeting the financial needs of its users.

The personal loan product was designed to assist consumers with debt consolidation, home renovation financing, and unforeseen expense coverage. Borrowell sought to reduce the stigma associated with borrowing and increase accessibility for a wider range of people by offering a clear and simple loan application process.

Credit Watch and Warnings

Borrowell added credit monitoring services to strengthen its value proposition further. By giving consumers immediate notifications when changes are made to their credit reports, this tool encourages them to be proactive and knowledgeable about their credit health. Credit monitoring has become a vital tool for consumers to guard against fraud and identity theft and track their credit score improvement efforts.

The launch of credit monitoring services evidently demonstrated Borrowell's dedication to offering complete financial solutions that enable people to take charge of their financial lives. It also emphasized the business's commitment to innovation and using technology to provide worthwhile services.

Utilizing Data and Technology: The Advantage of AI

One of Borrowell's unique selling points is its personalized financial solutions that leverage data and technology. A significant milestone in Borrowell's journey was the introduction of Molly, an AI-powered financial coach. Molly analyzes customer financial data using machine learning algorithms and offers personalized recommendations for debt management, credit score enhancement, and cost-cutting. Molly's role in providing tailored financial advice to Borrowell's users is a testament to the company's commitment to innovation and its mission to empower consumers with the information and resources they need to manage their money more wisely.

Since each user's financial behaviors and patterns are unique, Molly's insights make her recommendations applicable and doable. With the aid of this tailored strategy, consumers are better able to make decisions and move closer to their financial objectives. The AI-powered financial advisor personifies Borrowell's dedication to innovation and its goal of providing consumers with the information and resources they need to manage their money more wisely.

Creating a Community of Financial Literates

Aside from its financial services and products, Borrowell is deeply committed to advancing financial literacy. The company invests in educational materials, such as a blog with articles on budgeting, investing, credit management, and saving. These resources are designed to empower users with the knowledge they need to make informed financial decisions.

Additionally, Borrowell works with government organizations, non-profits, and educational institutions to expand its audience and improve financial literacy in Canada. By participating in community projects and educational activities, Borrowell hopes to improve financial education and give more people the tools they need to take charge of their economic destinies.

Collaborations and Partnerships

Over the years, Borrowell has strategically partnered with several companies to expand its reach and service offerings. These partnerships, which include financial institutions, IT firms, and educational institutions, are all aimed at enhancing the value that Borrowell provides to its users while advancing the company's mission of financial empowerment.

For example, Borrowell's collaboration with CIBC (Canadian Imperial Bank of Commerce) facilitated the company's ability to provide customers with an expanded array of financial services and products. This partnership also showed how fintech businesses and conventional banks may cooperate to enhance customer financial services.

Honors and Acknowledgments

Thanks to its innovative thinking and unwavering commitment to its goals, Borrowell has garnered numerous accolades and recognition in the fintech sector. The company has been lauded for its contributions to customer service, financial literacy, and financial technology. These accolades not only validate Borrowell's efforts but also instill confidence in its credibility and commitment to excellence.

Among the noteworthy honors and accolades are:

The Canadian FinTech & AI Awards' FinTech Company of the Year, Deloitte's Technology Fast 50, and KPMG's Top 50 Fintech Companies

These honors are a testament to Borrowell's influence on the fintech scene and its contribution to the development of financial services in Canada.

Borrowell: A Prominent Fintech Pioneer Presently, Borrowell is among Canada's top fintech firms, catering to millions of consumers nationwide. The company's platform has developed into various financial services and tools, including personal loans, credit monitoring, free credit reports and scores, and tailored financial counseling.

The company's user base keeps expanding because of Borrowell's unwavering focus on innovation, customer service, and financial empowerment. The company is still dedicated to its goal of assisting consumers in making wise credit and personal financial decisions and is always looking for new ways to use data and technology to improve its offerings.

The prospects for Borrowell

Borrowell is still committed to innovation and expansion as it looks to the future. As the fintech industry changes constantly, Borrowell is determined to stay ahead of the curve. Future advancements are possible for new financial products, enhanced credit monitoring tools, and more instructional resources.

In addition, Borrowell sees itself reaching outside of Canada and entering new markets with its cutting-edge financial services. Thanks to its commitment to its mission and its users, the company will remain a pioneer in the fintech sector, bringing about positive change and enabling people to take charge of their financial lives.

In synopsis, the trajectory of Borrowell, from its founding to its current position as a preeminent fintech enterprise, bears witness to the vision of its founders and the company's unwavering dedication to its objectives. Borrowell has enabled millions of Canadians to take charge of their financial destiny by filling a significant financial literacy gap and offering easily accessible and customized financial solutions.

A significant factor in the company's success has been its creative use of technology, strategic alliances, and customer-focused approach. As Borrowell expands and changes, it never wavers from its fundamental goal of financial empowerment—giving people the information and resources they need to make wise financial decisions.

In determination, Borrowell is more than just a fintech business—it is a driving force behind financial empowerment, providing a platform that blends data, technology, and human knowledge to provide all-encompassing financial solutions. By fostering innovation, openness, and financial literacy, Borrowell is influencing the direction of personal finance and assisting people in reaching their financial objectives.

Goals and objectives

Borrowell's unwavering commitment to financial empowerment and innovation is evident and appealing. The company's goal is to assist individuals in making wise credit decisions, a mission that guides everything the business does. From creating cutting-edge financial solutions to offering easily accessible learning materials, Borrowell's aim is to give everyone equal access to credit information and the tools they need to take charge of their financial destiny. This purpose was born out of a profound awareness of the difficulties many Canadians encounter while trying to manage their finances and credit.

The Mission's Beginnings

The founders of Borrowell saw the pervasive problems with credit management and financial literacy in Canada, which motivated the company's goal. The co-founders of Borrowell, Andrew Graham and Eva Wong, saw that many Canadians needed help to obtain their credit reports and, as a result, found it challenging to make wise financial decisions. They recognized a chance to develop a platform that would give consumers quick and easy access to credit reports and scores and tailored guidance to help them become better financial citizens.

The idea behind this vision was the conviction that every individual should have the opportunity to comprehend and adequately manage their credit. Borrowell's goal is to empower people with the information and resources they need to take charge of their financial lives, not simply data. Borrowell wants to remove obstacles and advance financial inclusion by facilitating the understanding and accessibility of financial information.

The Prospect: A Post-Financial Empowerment World

Borrowell's vision envisions a future where everyone has access to the resources and information they need to improve their financial situation. This ambitious goal includes a world where everyone is financially literate and can confidently make well-informed financial decisions. In Borrowell's ideal society, everyone has access to sound financial management regardless of background or economic standing.

Strategic Elements Underpinning the Goal

To realize its mission and vision, Borrowell has developed a strategic approach that underpins its operations and developments. This approach is based on several pillars, including:

To realize this goal, Borrowell bases its operations and developments on several strategic pillars, including:

1. Availability

Borrowell prioritizes making financial tools and information available to anyone. This entails offering free credit reports and ratings, user-friendly digital platforms, and materials suitable for a wide range of users. Another aspect of accessibility is ensuring that Borrowell's services are accessible to people in a variety of financial situations and geographical areas.

2. Openness

At Borrowell, openness is a fundamental principle. The organization is committed to giving its customers accurate and frank information so that they can better understand their credit scores, the variables influencing them, and the actions they can take to improve their financial situation. This openness extends to Borrowell's business procedures, guaranteeing that customers can rely on the advice and assistance offered.

3. Inventiveness

Borrowell's approach to financial services is characterized by an innovative mindset. Using technology and data analytics, Borrowell continually creates new tools and features to satisfy its users' changing demands. The company's dedication to innovation guarantees that it will always be at the forefront of the fintech sector, providing users with innovative solutions that give them power.

4. Pedagogy

Borrowell's commitment to financial education is unwavering. We offer a wealth of tools, from guides and articles to personalized guidance, to help consumers understand and manage their finances. By promoting financial literacy, Borrowell equips people with the knowledge they need to take control of their financial destinies and make informed decisions.

5. Social

Borrowell's primary goal is to create a financially savvy community. The business interacts with its users via various platforms, including social media, webinars, and alliances with non-profit organizations and educational institutions. Borrowell hopes to establish a community encouraging people to share their experiences and expertise in a caring setting.

Realizing the mission and vision

Borrowell's innovative products and services are instrumental in realizing our goals and mission. Each product is designed to empower customers financially and give them the confidence to manage their financial situations.

Free Credit Report and Score

Borrowell's main offering is free credit reporting and score access. This service is based on the company's goal to democratize credit information. Borrowell provides consumers with accurate and trustworthy credit data through a partnership with Equifax, one of the biggest credit bureaus. Consumers can track changes in their credit scores and comprehend the variables affecting their credit health by receiving weekly updates on their credit scores.

This program offers helpful information and gives consumers a head start on taking charge of their finances. By being aware of the factors that affect their credit score, users can take proactive actions to enhance their financial health and make educated judgments.

Individual Loans

With a focus on accessibility and openness, Borrowell provides personal loans to empower people to make wise credit decisions. Our use of technology expedites the application process, ensuring swift and effective creditworthiness determination. Borrowell's personal loans cater to a variety of needs, from home renovations to debt relief and unexpected expenses.

Borrowell offers a practical and user-friendly substitute for traditional lending with reasonable interest rates and customizable terms. The company's approach to personal loans demonstrates its dedication to providing consumers with the resources they require to manage their finances successfully.

Credit Management

A crucial part of Borrowell's goal to encourage financial health is its credit monitoring service. This service helps users stay informed and take appropriate action by receiving real-time alerts regarding changes to their credit report. Credit monitoring is an essential tool for tracking credit score improvement and safeguarding against fraud and identity theft.

By providing this service, Borrowell enables customers to take charge of their credit situation and make prompt decisions to improve their financial situation. The company's emphasis on credit monitoring demonstrates its commitment to offering complete financial solutions that meet the needs of its clients.

AI-Powered Financial Coach: Borrowell's AI-powered financial coach, Molly Molly, personifies the business's dedication to cutting-edge technology and individualized financial guidance. Molly evaluates user financial data and offers personalized advice and insights to help customers reduce debt, raise credit ratings, and save money. With this tailored approach, users find money management more manageable and approachable.

Molly offers relevant and meaningful recommendations based on each person's unique financial habits and trends. Borrowell provides an exceptional and worthwhile service by utilizing machine learning and data analytics, which aligns with its goal of enabling customers to make wise financial decisions.

Resources and Initiatives for Education

Borrowell has demonstrated its dedication to financial education through various resources and projects to advance financial literacy. The company blog covers a wide range of subjects, including investing and saving, managing credit, and budgeting. The articles' simple writing style allows a wide readership to grasp complicated financial ideas.

Borrowell provides webinars and workshops that offer in-depth knowledge on various financial subjects in addition to its blog. During these interactive events, participants can interact with financial professionals and ask questions. By providing these educational tools, Borrowell assists users in gaining a solid foundation in finance, empowering them to take charge of their financial destinies and make wise decisions.

Strategic Alliances for Increased Effect

To achieve its goals, Borrowell has established strategic alliances with several organizations. These partnerships broaden Borrowell's customer base and improve the services the company offers. Among the noteworthy alliances are:

Equifax

Thanks to its collaboration with one of the top credit bureaus, Equifax, Borrowell can offer its customers accurate and trustworthy credit reports and ratings. This partnership demonstrates Borrowell's dedication to truth and openness in its offerings.

CIBC Borrowell can provide its customers access to more financial services and products through its partnership with the Canadian Imperial Bank of Commerce. This collaboration also shows how fintech firms and conventional banks may cooperate to enhance customer financial services.

Academic Establishments and Non-Profits

Borrowell collaborates with academic institutions and non-profit groups to spread financial awareness and reach more people. These partnerships entail cooperative projects, such as training sessions, seminars, and workshops, aiming to improve financial literacy and enable them to manage their money.

Acknowledging Achievements and Medals

Many honors and accomplishments in the fintech sector attest to Borrowell's commitment to its goals and vision. These honors testify to the company's achievements and motivation to keep developing and aiming for greatness. Among the noteworthy honors and accolades are:

The Canadian FinTech & AI Awards' FinTech Company of the Year, Deloitte's Technology Fast 50, and KPMG's Top 50 Fintech Companies

These honors are a testament to Borrowell's influence on the fintech scene and its contribution to the development of financial services in Canada.

The Promise of Borrowell to Always Improve

Borrowell's mission and vision drive its dedication to ongoing development. The business constantly seeks new methods to improve its offerings and give customers more value. Possible future advancements include new financial products, enhanced credit monitoring tools, and more instructional resources.

Because of its commitment to innovation, Borrowell can stay at the forefront of the fintech sector and adapt to its user's changing needs over time. The organization will continue to direct its efforts toward a future where everyone has access to financial health by keeping accessibility, openness, and education as top priorities.

A Community-Based Strategy

Building a community around financial empowerment is crucial to Borrowell's goal and vision beyond simply offering financial products and services. The company interacts with its users through various platforms, encouraging a sense of support and community. Borrowell's user base is invaluable for exchanging expertise, firsthand accounts, and advice around credit and personal budgeting.

Borrowell allows people to interact and share knowledge utilizing social media, forums, and interactive events. In addition to increasing user involvement, this community-centric strategy supports Borrowell's objective of advancing financial empowerment and literacy.

The prospects for Borrowell

Borrowell is keeping its goals and vision front and center as it looks to the future. Borrowell aims to stay ahead of these changes, as the fintech landscape is ever-changing. Potential future developments could be:

- Growth into New Markets: To assist more people in achieving financial empowerment, Borrowell may consider expanding its cutting-edge financial services outside of Canada.

- New Financial Products: To better meet its customers' changing demands, the corporation might create new financial products that strengthen its value offer.

- Advanced services for credit monitoring: Borrowell has the potential to roll out additional credit monitoring services, giving consumers even more control over the state of their credit.

- Increased instructional resources: Borrowell might continue to add more in-depth manuals, interactive tools, and tailored guidance to its instructional offerings.

According to Borrowell, universal financial literacy will be achieved in the future, and people will be able to confidently make well-informed financial decisions. The company will remain a pioneer in the fintech sector, bringing about positive change and enabling people to take charge of their financial destinies, thanks to its dedication to innovation, transparency, and education.

The main factors influencing Borrowell's success and influence in the fintech sector are its goals and vision. By emphasizing innovation, accessibility, openness, education, and community, Borrowell enables people to make wise financial and credit choices. The organization stays a reliable partner in its users' financial journeys because of its commitment to its goals and vision.

Through its cutting-edge goods and services, astute alliances, and dedication to financial literacy, Borrowell is influencing the direction of personal finance and assisting people in reaching their financial objectives. The company's goal and vision are not only declarations but also catalysts for innovation and quality in all that Borrowell undertakes.

Borrowell is a platform that combines technology, data, and human expertise to create comprehensive financial solutions, making it more than just a fintech firm. It is a driving force behind financial emancipation. By staying true to its mission and vision, Borrowell is contributing to the creation of a world where everyone has the resources and information necessary to enhance their financial well-being and realize their financial goals.

Chapter Two: Free Credit Report and Score

Your credit score is more than simply a number in the modern financial world; it is an essential component of your identity. This three-digit number represents your creditworthiness and has a big impact on many different aspects of your financial life, such as credit card interest rates and loan approvals. While a lower score may limit your options and drive up your expenses, a higher score can lead to better financial chances.

Achieving your financial objectives and preserving your financial health depend on knowing and controlling your credit score. Thankfully, Borrowell simplifies this procedure by providing free access to your credit record and score. The purpose of this service is to give you the knowledge you need to make wise decisions and raise your credit score.

Everything You Should Know About Your Credit Report

It is crucial to comprehend the definition of your credit score and its calculation before learning how to obtain your free credit score. Based on your credit history, your credit score is a numerical indication of your creditworthiness. This comprises elements like:

- Your credit score is primarily based on your payment history. It displays your history of timely bill payments for credit cards, loans, and other financial commitments.

- Credit utilization is the percentage of your credit limits on your credit card balances as of right now. A reduced ratio suggests that you are making responsible use of credit.

- **Credit History:** The duration of your credit accounts impacts your credit score. Since a more extensive credit history gives more information about your credit activity, it usually results in a higher score.

- **Types of Credit Accounts:** A variety of credit accounts, including retail, installment, and credit card accounts, can raise your credit score.

- **Recent Credit Inquiries:** Your credit report receives a hard inquiry whenever you seek new credit. Frequently challenging questions can lower your score.

By being aware of these components, you can better understand your credit score and take action to raise it. Let us examine how using Borrowell to obtain your credit report and the score is simple.

How to Use Borrowell to View Your Free Credit Score Step-by-Step

Step 1: Open an account with Borrowell

You must first register for a Borrowell account to view your free credit score. This is a straightforward method that needs a few fundamental bits of information:

- **Scan the above QR code to get to Borrowell's website:** Navigate to the official Borrowell website and select the option to "Sign Up" or "Get Your Free Credit Score."

- **Provide personal information:** Set a password and enter your name and email address. You must also provide personal information, such as your address, date of birth, and Social Insurance Number (SIN), to verify your identification.

- **Accept the terms and conditions:** Examine Borrowell's privacy statement and terms and conditions. You permit Borrowell to access your credit information by accepting these.

- **Finalize your registration:** Enter your registration information to create your account. Before continuing, you should confirm your email address.

Step 2: Verify your identity.

After creating your account, you must authenticate yourself to ensure that the credit information being accessed is yours. This vital step is necessary to ensure accurate reporting and safeguard your personal information.

- Give further details: In order to confirm your identification, Borrowell might need further information from you, such as your driver's license number or recent bank statements.

- You may need to respond to security inquiries about your financial background. These inquiries help prove that the credit report legally belongs to you.

- Finish Verification: Adhere to the guidelines to complete the identity verification procedure. This stage could entail providing information about your credit history or downloading documents.

Step 3: View Your Report and Credit Score

You can use your Borrowell account to obtain your free credit report and score upon identity verification. Here's how to do it:

- Enter your account. Login: To access your Borrowell account, enter your password and email address.

- Locate your credit score by navigating: Locate the "Credit Report" or "Credit Score" area on your dashboard. You may see your credit score and a comprehensive report in this section.

- Examine Your Credit Report: It contains details about your credit accounts, past payments, credit inquiries, and any private or public records or collections. Spend some time going over each section in detail.

- Recognize Your Credit Score: Borrowell explains credit scores and the variables that affect them. Use this data to assess your current situation and pinpoint areas that require development.

Step 4: Keep an Eye on Your Credit Rating Frequently

Getting your credit score is only the first step. It is critical to check your credit to manage it well frequently. To assist you in maintaining your credit health, Borrowell provides the following tools and resources:

- Create Alerts: Borrowell offers credit monitoring services that enable you to receive notifications when your credit report changes. These alerts help you stay updated about new accounts, inquiries, and other fraud indicators.

- Monitor Your Progress: Utilize Borrowell's tools to monitor your credit score over time. By checking your score regularly, you can assess the effects of your financial practices and make the required corrections.

- Get Financial Advice: Borrowell provides tailored financial advice based on your credit history. With the help of these pointers, you can reach your financial objectives and raise your credit score.

Getting Your Free Credit Score Has Its Advantages

There are many reasons to use Borrowell to get your credit report and score:

1. Information-Based Empowerment

Knowing your credit score gives you essential knowledge about your financial situation. You can take charge of your financial destiny and make wise decisions if you know the elements that affect your credit score.

2. Better Budgeting

Knowing your credit score can help you prepare when making significant financial decisions, like applying for a credit card, mortgage, or auto loan. Knowing your creditworthiness can also help you select the best financial solutions and bargain for better conditions.

3. Early Fraud and Error Detection

You can identify any mistakes or fraudulent activities by routinely checking your credit report. Early detection and correction of errors can avert problems and safeguard the integrity of your credit.

4. Room for Development

By looking up your credit score, you can see exactly where you stand and where you need to improve. You can use this information to create a plan to raise your credit score and strengthen your finances.

Commonly Asked Questions

1. Is it genuinely accessible to view my credit score via Borrowell?

You may view your credit report and score for free using Borrowell. This service is free of any additional costs or hidden fees.

2. How frequently can I use Borrowell to check my credit score?

Borrowell allows you to check your credit score as frequently as possible. The company also sends you information weekly to keep you updated on any changes to your credit profile.

3. How does examining my credit score impact my credit score?

Actually, using Borrowell to check your credit score is a straightforward inquiry and will not impact your score. Reviewing your credit with soft inquiries keeps your creditworthiness unaffected.

4. How should I proceed if my credit report contains an error?

If you discover a mistake on your credit report, you should dispute the information by contacting either the credit bureau or Borrowell's customer service. Provide any supporting records you have to help fix the problem.

5. How can I raise my credit rating?

Paying your bills on time, lowering credit card balances, preventing new hard inquiries, and keeping various credit accounts are just a few tactics to raise your credit score. Personalized financial advice from Borrowell can offer direction on particular steps to follow.

Using Borrowell to get your free credit report and score is a significant step toward financial empowerment. Knowing your credit score and the variables that affect it will help you protect yourself from fraud, make wise decisions, and strengthen your financial situation.

With helpful tools and information to support your financial path, Borrowell's user-friendly platform makes obtaining and managing your credit score simple. Borrowell offers the knowledge and assistance you require, whether your goal is to raise your credit score, make critical financial plans, or keep up with your credit situation.

In closing, using Borrowell to get your free credit score is a simple and helpful procedure. This program allows you to take charge of your financial destiny, make wise decisions, and confidently work toward reaching your financial objectives.

Comprehending Your Credit Report

A credit report is a thorough account of your financial activities and credit history that provides a broad picture of your creditworthiness. Lenders, landlords, and other financial institutions utilize it as a crucial tool to evaluate your creditworthiness. It is essential to comprehend your credit report to manage it wisely and make wise financial decisions. This chapter will examine the many parts of a credit report, how to read it, and the implications for your financial situation.

A Credit Report: What Is It?

A credit report is a written summary of your credit history, including payment history, credit account details, and other pertinent financial data. Credit bureaus in North America (Equifax, Experian, and TransUnion) compile it using data from lenders and creditors. Your credit score, which represents your general creditworthiness, is determined using information from your credit report.

Items Included in a Credit Report

Familiarizing yourself with the various areas of your credit report is necessary to understand it. You can learn different things about your credit behavior from each section of your report. Below is a summary of the key elements:

1. Individual Data

This part contains some fundamental information about you, like:

- Name: Your entire given name.
- Address: Both your past and present addresses.
- Date of Birth: The day you were born.
- The Social Security Number (SIN) is a tool for confirming identity.
- Employer Details: Your position and employer as of right now, if applicable.

Visit the personal information area to confirm your identification and ensure the credit report is yours. It is critical to check the accuracy of this area because inaccurate information may result in problems obtaining credit or identity theft.

2. Accounts credit

You may get comprehensive details on your credit accounts in this section, which includes:

- Credit Cards: Information on every credit card account, such as the balance, credit limit, issuer, and account number.

- Loans: This section provides details about your outstanding student, vehicle, and mortgage loans. It covers the loan amount, the lender, the terms of repayment, and the remaining balance.

- Retail Accounts: Account information and payment history for accounts with retail establishments.

Every account listing consists of:

- Account Status: Indicates if the account is in collections, closed, or open.

- Payment History: The account's payments, including late or delinquent payments.

- Credit utilization, which impacts your credit score, is the ratio of your credit limit to your current debt on credit cards.

Knowing your credit accounts allows you to better control your payment history and credit use, two crucial aspects of your credit score.

3. Credit Reports

Lenders and other organizations may request access to your credit record through credit inquiries. There are two categories of questions:

- Hard Inquiries happen when you apply for a loan or new credit. Hard inquiries can lower your credit score, mainly if they occur frequently in a short time.

- When you examine your credit report, or a lender looks through your credit for pre-approval offers, these are known as soft inquiries. Your credit score is unaffected by soft inquiries.

By reviewing your credit inquiries, you can monitor how frequently people have accessed your credit report and spot any unauthorized requests that might indicate fraud.

4. Open documents

This section contains public record information that may have an impact on your creditworthiness, including:

- Bankruptcies: Information about any filed bankruptcy cases, such as the type of case and the filing date.

- Judgments: court orders imposed on you for outstanding debts.

- Liens: property rights resulting from delinquent payments.

You should monitor public records carefully since they might significantly affect your credit score. It is imperative to swiftly correct any inaccuracies or obsolete information.

5. Collections

The following will be included in this area if you have any accounts that have been forwarded to collections:

- Accounts under Collection: Details about accounts that have been turned over to a collection agency as a result of nonpayment.
- Details of the collection process include the amount due, the agency name, and the date the account was referred to collections.

If you have collection accounts, your credit score may suffer. It is vital to resolve any collection accounts and ensure the reports are accurate.

How to Understand Your Credit Report

Understanding how each part affects your creditworthiness is essential to interpreting your credit report. Here are some important things to think about:

1. Examine your past payment records.

The most critical component of your credit score is your payment history. While late payments or defaults might lower your score, a history of on-time payments has a favorable impact. Examine each account's payment history to ensure it is accurate and address any inconsistencies.

2. Examine your credit utilization.

The ratio of your credit card balances to your credit limits is known as credit usage. When your credit usage ratio is lower, it suggests that you are managing your credit well. To maintain a good credit score, keep your credit utilization percentage below 30% of your overall credit limit.

3. Keep an eye on your credit accounts.

Check your credit accounts regularly to ensure accurate information. Look into any accounts you do not recognize; these could be indicators of identity theft. Ensure your account balances are correct and that closed accounts are recorded.

4. Examine your credit reports.

Look for any complex queries that can affect your credit rating. A few questions have little impact, but several quick inquiries can be harmful. Look into any unsanctioned questions you come across right away.

5. Talk about public collections and records.

Collection accounts and public records have a significant impact on your credit score. Examine these parts thoroughly, and then address any problems that you see. Contact the credit bureau to fix any mistakes in your public records.

What to Do If You Discover Errors

Discovering mistakes on your credit report might be unsettling, but quickly fixing them can help keep your credit in good standing. If you come across errors, you should take the following actions:

1. Compile records

Gather any supporting evidence that clarifies the inaccuracy on your credit report. Receipts, account statements, and correspondence with creditors are examples of this.

2. Speak with the credit bureau.

Submit a dispute to the credit reporting agency that provided the report. You can do this over the phone, via mail, or online. Describe the error in full and attach any relevant files.

3. Speak with the debtor.

Speak with the lender or creditor who provided the false information. Describe the problem and offer any supporting data. Ask them to update the credit bureau and correct the information.

4. Confirmation

Keep an eye on your credit record to ensure the mistake is fixed. The credit bureau must investigate complaints and offer a response within 30 days. If necessary, follow up to ensure the problem has been fixed.

Your Credit Report's Effect on Financial Decisions

When making many financial decisions, your credit report is essential. These decisions include:

1. Applications for Credit and Loans

When you apply for a loan or credit card, lenders examine your credit report to determine how creditworthy you are. An approval with better terms, including reduced lending rates, is more likely when your credit report is positive.

2. Hiring an Apartment

When you apply for a property, landlords may review your credit report. A clean credit record may help you get a rental and may also impact the conditions of your lease.

3. Premiums for insurance

Some insurance firms consult credit reports when determining insurance rates. A good credit report could result in lower premiums, while a bad credit record could result in higher expenses.

4. Job Possibilities

Certain employers could check your credit report as part of the recruiting process, particularly for jobs involving financial responsibility. Your chances of finding work may improve if your credit report is spotless.

Techniques for Keeping Your Credit Report in Good Shape

A clean credit record requires aggressive management and regular financial practices. The following are some tips to maintain the integrity of your credit report:

1. Make timely bill payments.

Paying bills on time is essential to maintaining a good payment history. Establish automated payments or reminders to make sure you always remember a deadline.

2. Control the Use of Credit

Avoid using all your credit limits on your credit cards, and keep your balances modest. Pay off current amounts and make responsible credit usage decisions to maintain a good credit utilization ratio.

3. Keep an eye on your credit. Frequently

To monitor your credit situation, periodically check your credit report. Borrowell's free credit monitoring services can help you spot possible problems and monitor modifications.

4. Create a wide-ranging credit portfolio.

Various credit accounts, including retail, installment, and credit card accounts, can improve your credit rating. To establish a solid credit history, use credit of all kinds sensibly.

5. Deal with negative things right away.

Take prompt action to resolve any adverse items that appear on your credit report, such as late payments or collection accounts. Collaborate with lenders to settle disputes and enhance your credit record.

You must be aware of your credit report to effectively manage your credit and make wise financial decisions. By becoming familiar with the elements of your credit report and learning how to understand them, you can take proactive measures to maintain a good credit profile.

With Borrowell's free credit score and report service, you can monitor your credit health and make wise financial decisions by learning essential details about your credit history. You may ensure that you meet your financial objectives and maintain a good credit profile by routinely checking your credit report and correcting any mistakes or unfavorable things.

To sum up, your credit report is an effective instrument for evaluating and monitoring your financial situation. By remaining informed and taking proactive steps, you can improve your creditworthiness, obtain greater financial prospects, and realize long-term financial success.

The advantages of weekly updates

In today's hectic financial world, monitoring your credit score and report is more critical than ever. Your credit score is crucial to your financial well-being, affecting everything from interest rates to loan approvals. Borrowell's weekly credit report and score updates are among its most beneficial features. This chapter explores the advantages of getting these regular updates and explains why maintaining and enhancing your credit health depends on them.

Weekly Updates: Their Significance

Credit reports and ratings change over time in response to your financial behavior. Weekly updates give you a constant and up-to-date picture of your credit situation, enabling you to monitor changes and respond promptly. Let us examine the particular advantages of getting weekly reports on your credit record and score.

1. Early Error Detection

Recognize errors quickly.

Errors can occur in credit reports. Errors in bookkeeping, out-of-date data, and even fraudulent activity can all lead to mistakes. Weekly updates allow you to identify disparities as soon as they arise and take appropriate action. Early detection will enable you to challenge errors before they adversely affect your credit score, such as when a new account you did not open or an inaccurately reported late payment shows up on your report.

Fixing Mistakes

You can quickly fix a problem as soon as you find it. This usually entails contacting the concerned creditor and the credit bureau to fix the problem. The sooner you fix errors, the less negative impact they will have on your credit score, preserving or improving your credit health.

2. Keeping an eye out for fraudulent activity

Remain alert for identity theft.

Fraud and identity theft can negatively impact your credit score. You may keep an eye on any odd activity on your credit report, such as new accounts or complex queries, with the help of weekly updates. You can intervene quickly to lessen the consequences and stop more harm if you see any suspicious activity.

Implementing preventive actions

With regular monitoring, you can set up fraud alerts or credit freezes if needed. These precautions can reduce the possibility of identity theft and safeguard your credit profile from unwanted access.

3. Monitoring Your Credit Development

Calculate the Effect of Financial Choices

With weekly updates, you may see how your financial decisions impact your credit score in real time. Observing how your credit score changes in response to debt reduction, credit limit increases, or account closures can assist you in determining which steps are best for enhancing your credit situation.

Adapt your strategies as necessary.

Monitoring the effects of your financial decisions can help you modify your financial plans according to what is working and what is not. For example, you can concentrate more on controlling your credit card balances if lowering your credit use raises your credit score.

4. Improving Budgetary Management

Get ready for significant financial changes.

Knowing your credit score is essential when making big financial decisions like purchasing a house or requesting a car loan. Weekly updates ensure you always know where you stand credit-wise, which helps you make better plans for these decisions.

Enhance credit conditions

Being aware of your credit score in real-time aids in your ability to bargain for better conditions on loans and credit products. You can use your good credit score to negotiate better loan terms or lower interest rates.

5. Establishing and Preserving a Good Credit Record

Encourage conscientious use of credit.

Reviewing your credit report on a regular basis promotes healthy credit usage. It can be inspiring to see your credit score rise due to sound financial practices, as it validates actions like timely bill payments and responsible credit management.

Determine which areas need improvement.

Weekly reports highlight things you can do to improve your credit profile. You can lower your balances and raise your credit score, for instance, if you observe a pattern of rising credit utilization.

6. Mental tranquility

Diminish your money worries.

One way to lessen financial concerns is to be aware of the regular updates you receive on your credit report and score. This knowledge can significantly reduce your worries about unforeseen changes to your credit profile, giving you more peace of mind when handling your finances.

Remain knowledgeable and resourceful.

Getting regular updates gives you the information you need to make wise decisions and take proactive measures to raise or maintain your credit score. This empowerment gives you more influence over your financial future.

How to Utilize Weekly Updates to Their Fullest

Weekly updates are only the first step in the process. Take into consideration the following advice to make the most of this feature:

Examine your report thoroughly.

When you get your weekly update, spend some time carefully reviewing your credit report. Check for any anomalies, mistakes, or modifications. Also, keep an eye on your credit inquiries, payment history, and credit accounts.

Monitor shifts over time.

Record your weekly updates so you can monitor changes over time. This can assist you in seeing patterns in your credit profile and comprehending how various activities affect your credit score.

Act Immediately

Acting immediately upon discovering any mistakes or indications of fraudulent conduct is crucial. To address problems and safeguard your credit health, it's important to get in touch with the credit bureau and your creditors promptly.

Utilize the knowledge for budgetary planning.

Use the data from your weekly updates to inform the planning and modification of your financial plans. With the help of these insights, you can make educated decisions, set objectives, and improve your credit management.

The Significance of Borrowell's Weekly Reports

For weekly updates on your credit score and report, Borrowell provides a feature-rich platform. Borrowell's platform stands out for its intuitive dashboard, personalized insights, timely notifications, and comprehensive educational tools. This is how Borrowell revolutionizes the way you monitor your credit.

An easy-to-use dashboard

Borrowell provides an intuitive dashboard for weekly credit updates. The platform's clear visualizations of your credit report and score make it easy to comprehend your credit status.

Individualized Perspectives

Based on your credit profile, Borrowell provides tailored insights and suggestions. These observations can help you comprehend the elements affecting your score and offer helpful suggestions for raising it.

Notifications and alerts

When something significant happens to your credit report, like a new account opening or a change in your credit score, Borrowell notifies you and sends alerts. By receiving these alerts, you may remain informed and respond promptly.

Teaching Materials

Borrowell provides an abundance of educational tools to maximize your weekly updates and better comprehend your credit report. Through interactive tools, articles, and tutorials, Borrowell offers helpful information to assist your financial path.

One of the most effective tools for monitoring and enhancing your credit health is getting weekly updates on your credit report and score. Frequent updates provide various advantages, such as early error identification, fraud monitoring, credit improvement tracking, improved financial planning, and upholding a clean credit history.

Borrowell's platform makes it easy to access and use these changes. It gives you the knowledge and resources you need to take charge of your credit report. By being aware and proactive, you can ensure that your credit is in good shape, lessen your financial anxiety, and confidently reach your financial objectives.

To sum up, the importance of weekly updates is immeasurable. They give you a constant picture of your credit situation, empowering you to take proactive measures to uphold and enhance your credit profile and make wise selections. With Borrowell's assistance, you may use routine credit monitoring to strengthen your financial position in the future.

Chapter Three: Making a Personal Loan Application

In today's financial environment, personal loans are a well-liked and adaptable choice for those looking to finance a range of purposes, from debt consolidation to a significant purchase. Comprehending the application process for a personal loan is vital to ensuring a seamless journey and obtaining the most favorable conditions. This chapter offers a thorough how-to for applying for a personal loan, including information on evaluating lenders, understanding loan terms, and preparing your application.

Comprehending personal loans

Before diving into the application process, it's crucial to grasp the concept of personal loans and how they function. A personal loan is an installment loan that involves a lump sum to be repaid over a set period, usually with fixed monthly installments. The choice between secured and unsecured personal loans is yours to make, but understanding the implications is key to making an informed decision.

Secured personal loans require an asset, such as a car or savings account, as security. Due to the lender's reduced risk, these loans frequently offer cheaper interest rates.

Unsecured Personal Loans Depend only on your creditworthiness; they do not need collateral. Because lenders face more risk, interest rates for unsecured loans are often higher.

Personal loans, with their versatility, can be a boon for various needs, from debt consolidation to home improvements and medical expenses. This flexibility makes them an attractive option for many borrowers, empowering them to meet their financial goals.

Ready to Submit a Personal Loan Application

Preparation is the cornerstone of a successful personal loan application. By taking the time to organize your financial information and understand your borrowing needs, you can significantly increase your chances of approval and secure favorable terms. This preparation should instill a sense of confidence in your ability to navigate the loan application process.

1. Evaluate your financial condition.

Scrutinize your financial status before applying for a personal loan. Think about taking these actions:

- **Analyze Your Credit Score:** Your credit score is largely dependent on your personal loan eligibility, including the interest rate and other terms.

- **Accuracy:** After obtaining a copy, check your credit report. If your score is not as high as you want it to be, work on raising it before applying.

- **Determine Your Ratio of Debt to Income:** Lenders evaluate your ability to repay the loan based on your debt-to-income (DTI) ratio. Divide your total monthly debt payments by your gross monthly income to find your DTI. A lower debt-to-income ratio raises your chances of approval and is a sign of more robust financial standing.

- **Calculate the Amount of Your Loan:** Determine how much money you need to borrow to ensure the amount you borrow is appropriate for your ability to repay it. Take out only the amount of debt you can afford to repay.

2. Compile the documentation required.

Having the necessary paperwork ready will make the application process go more smoothly. Lenders frequently seek the following documents:

- Government-issued identification, such as a passport or driver's license, is proof of identity.

- Proof of Income: To confirm your income, please provide recent pay stubs, tax returns, or bank statements.

- Employer contact details or an employment letter serve as employment verification.

- Credit Report: A copy of your credit report may be required by some lenders.

- Bank Statements: Accounts from the last few months demonstrate your financial standing.

3. Examine possible lenders.

For personal loans, not all lenders provide the same terms and conditions. To discover the ideal lender for your needs, research different lenders, such as banks, credit unions, and online lenders. Take into account the following elements:

- **Interest Rates:** Compare interest rates to find the most affordable option. A lower interest rate will lower the total cost of the loan.

- **Charges:** Pay attention to any loan-related costs, including origination, late, and prepayment penalties.

- **Loan Terms:** Examine the repayment terms, such as the loan's duration and monthly payment amounts.

- **Client Testimonials:** Read other borrowers' reviews and ratings to evaluate the lender's reputation and customer service.

The Procedure for Applications

You can begin the application procedure whenever you are ready. This section will walk you through every process stage, from applying to getting the money.

1. Completing the application

Filling out the application is the first step in the personal loan application process. Depending on the lender, you can complete this online or in person. Be ready to share comprehensive details regarding your financial circumstances, such as:

- Name, residence, birth date, and phone number are examples of personal information.

- Employment Details: income, job title, duration of employment, and current employer.

- Loan Specifics: the loan's intended use and the amount you want to borrow.

- Financial Information: Specifics regarding your earnings, outlays, and outstanding debts.

2. Document Submission

Once you have finished the application, you must submit the necessary paperwork. This usually consists of bank statements, identification documentation, and income verification. Make sure that all documentation is correct and current to prevent delays in the approval process.

3. Pending Authorization

After you submit your application and supporting documents, the lender will check your information. This could entail verifying your financial information and running a credit check. The length of the approval procedure varies based on the lender and the intricacy of your application; it might take a few hours to several days.

4. Getting Loan Offers

If the lender approves your application, you will get loan offers. These offers will detail the loan amount, interest rate, repayment conditions, and related costs. To choose which deal best suits your needs, take the time to examine and contrast each one thoroughly.

5. Taking Up a Loan Offer

After reviewing the loan offers, decide which one best suits your requirements and agree to the terms. A loan agreement containing the terms and conditions of the loan is typically required for this. Before you sign, be sure you understand the agreement thoroughly.

6. Getting Paid

The lender will transfer the money to your bank account once you accept a loan offer and sign the contract. Though it usually happens within a few business days, the time it takes to receive the funds can vary. You can use the money for its intended purpose as soon as it is placed.

A Successful Personal Loan Application: Some Advice

If you use these pointers to improve your chances of acceptance and negotiate favorable terms, getting a personal loan can be a simple process:

1. Keep your credit score high.

One of the most crucial elements in getting a personal loan with good terms is having a high credit score. To keep your credit score high:

- **Pay Bills on Time:** Paying your bills on time every time shows that you are a responsible financial citizen.

- **Keep Balances Low:** Keep your credit card balances below your credit limit.

- **Prevent Needless Credit Inquiries:** To prevent several hard inquiries on your credit report, keep the number of credit applications you make to a minimum.

2. Present a consistent income

Borrowers must have a steady source of income to be eligible for a loan. Ensure your income is accurately recorded, and consider adding any extra money from bonuses or side gigs.

3. Cut down on current debt

Excessive current debt may harm your loan application. Prior to applying for a personal loan, concentrate on paying off current debts to reduce your debt-to-income ratio.

4. Select the appropriate lender.

The conditions and qualifications for personal loans vary among lenders. To get the best interest rate, fees, and loan terms for your circumstances, compare the offers from several lenders.

5. Be truthful and precise.

Give true and precise facts on your loan application. Providing false information may result in rejection, delays, or even legal repercussions.

Typical Obstacles and How to Get Past Them

Applying for a personal loan might be difficult at times. However, you can improve your chances of success by being aware of these obstacles and learning how to overcome them.

1. A low credit score

A low credit score may result in higher interest rates or make it more challenging to get a personal loan. To get over this:

- **Strive to Raise Your Credit Score:** Pay off current obligations, correct any necessary errors in your credit report, and avoid late payments.

- **Examine Secured Credit:** If you have valuable assets, you might be able to get a secured loan even with a lower credit score.

2. A high ratio of debt to income

A high debt-to-income ratio suggests you devote a sizeable amount of your income to servicing your current debt. To raise your ratio:

- **Reduce Debt:** To lessen your total debt, concentrate on paying off high-interest loans.
- **Boost Income:** Seek chances to boost your earnings, including taking on more jobs or requesting a raise.

3. Insufficient Records

You risk having your loan application denied or delayed if you do not provide the required paperwork. To steer clear of this:

- **Plan:** Obtain the necessary paperwork before beginning the application process.
- **Maintain Ordered Records:** Structure your records to guarantee that your financial paperwork is easily accessible when needed.

The Value of Evaluating Different Loan Offers

Securing the best terms requires comparing loan offers from several lenders. This is the reason why:

1. Rates of Interest

Interest rates differ among lenders according to how well they judge your creditworthiness. Over time, even a slight variation in interest rates can significantly affect the loan's overall cost.

2. Costs Lenders might differ significantly in their origination, late payment, and prepayment penalty costs. You can determine the actual cost of the loan by comparing these costs.

3. Conditions of Repayment

Lenders may have different terms for loan repayment, such as loan length and monthly payment amounts. Select terms based on your ability to repay and your financial objectives.

4. Client Support

Good customer service can make the loan application procedure run more smoothly and transparently. Reading reviews and ratings can help you learn more about the quality of the lender's customer service.

Making an extensive financial choice, like applying for a personal loan, requires serious planning and thought. However, you can improve your chances of getting a personal loan with good terms by being aware of the application procedure, preparing your financial documents, and evaluating loan offers.

To increase your application's chances of approval, keep your credit score high, provide proof of steady income, and pay off any debt you may have. Apply with accuracy and sincerity, and select a lender whose terms and rates are reasonable and meet your requirements.

Personal loans can give you the financial flexibility you need to accomplish your objectives, whether paying off debt, saving for a big purchase, or facing unforeseen costs. If you are prepared and knowledgeable, you may complete the application procedure and obtain the money you require to support your financial journey.

Loan Term and Interest Rates

Empower yourself in the personal loan landscape by mastering the crucial elements of loan terms and interest rates. These two factors are the key to understanding your borrowing costs and conditions. This guide will delve into the nuances of loan conditions and interest rates, equipping you with the knowledge to make informed decisions when applying for a personal loan.

Understanding loan duration

Loan terms describe the specific conditions under which a loan is given and repaid. These terms are detailed in the loan agreement and can differ significantly between lenders and loan packages. Loan conditions include the loan amount, payback period, monthly installments, and applicable fees.

1. Loan Amount.

The loan amount is the total amount you borrow from a lender. Personal loans can range from a few hundred dollars to several tens of thousands, depending on the lender's criteria and your creditworthiness. Borrowing only what you need is critical to preventing needless debt and interest payments.

2. Repayment Period

The payback duration, often known as the loan term, refers to how long you must repay the debt. Personal loans frequently have repayment durations ranging from one to seven years. Shorter repayment durations usually mean larger monthly payments but lower total interest expenses. On the other hand, longer payback durations result in lower monthly payments but higher total loan interest expenses over time.

3. Monthly payments.

Monthly payments are the predetermined sums you pay monthly to repay your debt. These payments depend on the loan amount, interest rate, and repayment duration. To avoid late payments or defaults, make sure your monthly payments fit within your budget.

4. Charges

Personal loans may have a variety of fees and levies, including:

- **Origination Fees:** The lender charges a one-time cost to handle the loan application. This fee is often a percentage of the loan amount, ranging from 1% to 8%.

- **Late Payment Fees:** Fees levied for failing to meet a payment deadline.

Prepayment penalties are fees for paying off a loan early that reimburse the lender for lost interest income.

Administrative fees are additional expenses for administering the loan account.

Understanding these fees is critical for determining the loan's actual cost and avoiding unexpected charges.

Interest rates are the cost of borrowing.

Interest rates represent the cost of borrowing money as a percentage of the loan amount. They play an essential part in deciding the overall cost of a personal loan. Interest rates can be fixed or variable, and various factors, such as your credit score, loan period, and market conditions, determine them.

1. Fixed versus variable interest rates

Fixed interest rates remain stable throughout the loan's term, resulting in predictable monthly payments. Fixed rates are appropriate for borrowers who desire stability and avoid the danger of rising interest rates.

Variable interest rates can fluctuate regularly depending on market conditions and are often linked to an index like the prime rate. Variable rates may begin lower than fixed rates but can rise over time, resulting in varying monthly costs. These rates are appropriate for borrowers who can handle some uncertainty and may benefit from lower initial rates.

2. Annual percentage rate (APR).

The annual percentage rate (APR) incorporates the interest rate and any loan-related fees, offering a more complete picture of the loan's cost. APR is important for comparing loan offers because it represents the actual cost of borrowing. A lower APR suggests a more inexpensive loan.

3. Factors influencing interest rates.

Several factors affect the interest rate you get on a personal loan:

- **Credit score:** Lenders use your credit score to determine your creditworthiness, which measures how likely you are to repay your debts. Higher credit scores are often associated with lower interest rates, but lower scores may result in higher rates.

- **Income and employment:** Stable income and employment history reflect your ability to repay the loan, which may result in lower interest rates.

- **Debt-to-Income Ratio:** A lower debt-to-income ratio implies better financial health, making you a lower-risk borrower who may qualify for lower interest rates.

- **Loan Amount and Terms:** Larger loan amounts and shorter repayment periods are frequently associated with lower interest rates, as they represent less risk for the lender.

How to get the best loan terms and interest rates.

Securing the best loan terms and interest rates necessitates meticulous planning and the comparison of several loan offers. *Here are some techniques to help you get favorable terms:*

1. Improve your credit score.

A credit score is one of the most critical considerations when calculating your interest rate. To boost your credit score:

- Paying bills on time displays financial responsibility and might help your credit score.

- **Reduce Debt:** Paying down existing debt reduces your debt-to-income ratio and increases your credit score.

- **Correct errors:** Check your credit report for errors and dispute any that could lower your score.
- **Limit New Credit Applications:** Attempting to open several new credit accounts quickly will damage your credit score.

2. Shop around and compare offers.

Proactivity is key when it comes to securing the best loan terms and interest rates. Different lenders offer different terms and interest rates. By shopping around and comparing loan offers, you can take control of your financial situation and ensure you're getting the best deal. Consider both traditional banks and online lenders, as the latter often provide competitive rates and more flexible terms.

3. Consider a secured loan.

Consider a secured loan if you have valuable assets, such as a car or a savings account. Secured loans often have lower interest rates than unsecured loans, which are not backed by collateral since the lender has collateral to mitigate risk.

4. Negotiate loan terms.

Feel free to negotiate loan conditions with your lender. If you have an excellent credit history and a positive relationship with your bank, you can negotiate better terms, such as a lower interest rate or fewer fees.

5. Go for shorter repayment periods.

Shorter payback terms result in larger monthly payments, but they can drastically reduce the overall interest paid over the life of the loan. If you can afford larger payments, switching to a shorter-term plan can save you money in the long run.

The Effect of Loan Terms and Interest Rates on Loan Costs

Understanding how loan terms and interest rates affect the total cost of a loan is critical for making sound borrowing decisions. Let us look at a few examples to demonstrate this influence.

1. Example 1: Comparison of Loan Terms

Consider a borrower who obtains a $10,000 personal loan at a fixed interest rate of 8%. Let us compare the overall cost of the loan over various repayment periods.

- 3-Year Loan Term
    - Monthly payment: $313.36.
    - Total interest paid: $1,281.00.
    - Total loan cost: $11,281.00.
- 5-Year Loan Term
    - Monthly payment: $202.76.

- Total interest paid: $2,165.60.
- Total Loan Cost: $12,165.60.

In this case, the borrower pays much less interest over the shorter 3-year term despite more outstanding monthly payments.

2. Example 2: Comparing Interest Rates.

Now, let's examine the entire cost of a $10,000 personal loan with a 5-year duration and various interest rates.

- 8% interest rate.
    - Monthly payment: $202.76.
    - Total interest paid: $2,165.60.
    - Total Loan Cost: $12,165.60.
- 12% interest rate.
    - Monthly payment: $222.44.
    - Total interest paid: $3,346.40.
    - Total Loan Cost: $13,346.40

In this instance, a higher interest rate results in a much larger overall loan cost, emphasizing the necessity of obtaining the lowest available rate.

Lenders' Role in Setting Loan Terms and Interest Rates

Lenders have a critical influence in deciding personal loan conditions and interest rates. Lenders have different procedures and standards for assessing borrowers. Understanding these distinctions might help you select the best lender for your needs.

1. Traditional banks.

Traditional banks often provide personal loans with competitive interest rates and various lending sizes and terms. They may have stricter eligibility restrictions, such as higher credit scores and more detailed documentation. Banks are an excellent choice for applicants with solid credit histories and established relationships with their financial institutions.

2. Credit unions

Credit unions are member-owned financial institutions that often offer personal loans with cheaper interest rates and costs than traditional banks. They may also provide more personalized service and flexible terms. Credit unions are a good choice for borrowers who are already members or can join.

3. Online lenders

Online lenders have become famous for personal loans due to their ease, quick approval processes, and cheap interest rates. These lenders may have more liberal eligibility requirements and can accommodate a more extensive range of credit profiles. Online lenders are an excellent option for borrowers who want a simple application process and quick funding.

4. Peer-to-peer (P2P) lenders.

P2P lending systems match borrowers with independent investors who fund personal loans. These platforms can provide competitive interest rates with customizable terms. P2P lenders may be more likely to cooperate with clients with low credit scores or unusual financial circumstances. They are a viable choice for borrowers seeking alternatives to traditional financial institutions.

Understanding loan terms and interest rates is critical for making sound decisions when applying for a personal loan. If you understand the components of loan terms, the factors that influence interest rates, and the tactics for obtaining favorable terms, you may confidently handle the borrowing process.

Remember to improve your credit score, shop around for the best deals, and evaluate how different loan terms and interest rates affect the overall cost of the loan. Whether you go with a traditional bank, credit union, internet lender, or peer-to-peer platform, comparing and understanding your alternatives will help you find a personal loan that suits your financial needs and goals.

Personal loans can give you the financial freedom you need for various objectives, including debt consolidation and funding significant expenses. With the correct information and preparation, you can maximize the benefits of this versatile financial tool and reach your financial goals.

Use Cases: Home renovations, debt consolidation, and more

Personal loans are flexible financial instruments with a multitude of applications. They allow borrowers to finance various requirements and endeavors, from major home renovations to consolidating high-interest debt. This chapter examines several typical use cases for personal loans to show you how they can be an effective tool for better managing and organizing your finances.

Consolidation of Debt

One of the most common justifications for obtaining a personal loan is debt consolidation. It entails streamlining your finances and saving you money on interest by merging several high-interest debts into a single loan with a lower interest rate.

1. Comprehending Debt Consolidation

Deb consolidation involves taking out a personal loan to pay off current debts, such as credit card balances, medical expenses, or other personal loans. Since the interest rate on the new loan is usually lower than that of the previous debt, there will be fewer monthly payments and a decrease in total interest expenses. This method will enable you to pay off your debt more quickly and effectively.

2. Advantages of Consolidating Debt

- **Reduced Interest Rates:** Unlike credit cards, personal loans frequently offer lower interest rates, which can result in substantial savings over time.

- **Simplified Payments:** Combining several loans into one may help you manage your money more efficiently and lower your chance of missing or being late with payments.

- **Reduction of High-Interest Credit Card Debt:** Reducing your credit utilization ratio will help raise your credit score.

- **Fixed Repayment Schedule:** Personal loans have set repayment terms, giving borrowers a precise deadline for paying off their debt.

3. How to Consolidate Debt Using a Personal Loan

Use a personal loan for debt consolidation in the following ways to make it work:

- **Examine Your Debt:** Determine the overall amount of debt you wish to pay off, as well as the interest rates and monthly installment amounts associated with each loan.

- **Compare loan Offers:** Look for personal loans with the best terms and lowest interest rates. Consider both offline and internet lenders.

- **Apply for the Loan:** Complete the loan application and send the necessary supporting documents. Be truthful about your financial circumstances to improve your chances of being accepted.

- **Pay Off Current Loans:** Use the proceeds to settle all your outstanding high-interest loans.

- **Handle Your New Loan:** Make consistent, on-time payments on your loan to preserve good credit and prevent taking on more debt.

Renovations in the House

Home renovations can significantly enhance your property's value, functionality, and aesthetic appeal. Personal loans provide a convenient way to finance these improvements, allowing you to upgrade your home without depleting your savings.

1. Home Improvement Project Types

Numerous home renovation projects, such as the following, can be financed with personal loans:

- **Kitchen remodels:** Creating a contemporary, helpful kitchen requires updating the worktops, cabinets, appliances, and flooring.

- **Bathroom renovations:** Adding lighting, tile, and fixtures will improve your bathroom's comfort and design.

- **Room additions:** Increase the number of bedrooms, bathrooms, or living areas to accommodate your expanding family.

- **Exterior Improvements:** To enhance your outdoor living area, build patios, decks, or gardens.

- **Energy Efficiency Improvements:** To lower utility expenses and raise the value of your house, install solar panels, insulation, or energy-efficient windows.

2. Advantages of Financing Home Renovations with a Personal Loan

- **Fast Funds Access:** Personal loans give you quick access to money to start your home renovation project immediately.

- **No Collateral Needed:** Unlike home equity loans, personal loans do not need your house as collateral, which lowers the possibility that you will forfeit it in the event of a default.

- **Fixed Interest Rates:** The fixed interest rates associated with personal loans facilitate easier monthly payment budgeting.

- **Boost Home Value:** Home upgrades can raise a property's resale value and yield a return on investment.

3. How to Use a Personal Loan to Finance Home Improvements

To use a personal loan to finance your home repair project, take these actions:

- **Plan your project:** Establish its parameters, including its budget and extent. Get quotes from contractors and draft a thorough plan.

- Examine and compare personal loan offers from several lenders, paying particular attention to interest rates, costs, and repayment terms.

- **Apply for the Loan:** Send your application and the required supporting paperwork. To bolster your application, include comprehensive project information.

- **Receive monies:** Once the Loan has been approved, the funds will be deposited into your bank account. You can use the money for supplies, labor, and other project-related costs.

- **Handle Your Loan**: Schedule your personal loan installments to avoid penalties and keep your credit score high.

Health care costs

Unexpected medical expenses can place a significant financial burden on individuals and families. Personal loans offer a flexible solution for covering these costs, including surgeries, treatments, and other expenses that may not be covered by insurance.

1. Typical Medical Costs Paid for by Personal Loans

Numerous medical costs can be paid for with personal loans, such as:

- Hospital stays, surgeries, and ER visits result in emergency medical bills.
- Major dental procedures include crowns, root canals, and orthodontics.
- **Cosmetic Surgery:** Non-insurance-covered elective surgeries.
- **Costs related to fertility treatments:** IVF and other fertility procedures.
- **Long-Term Care costs include** nursing home, assisted living, or home health care.

2. Advantages of Paying for Medical Bills with a Personal Loan

- **Quick Access to Funds:** Personal loans give you immediate access to money to cover medical costs.

- **Flexible Use:** The money is available to cover medical bills, allowing patients to pay for care.

- **No Collateral Required:** Since personal loans do not need collateral, there is less risk involved in borrowing.

- **Fixed Payments:** It is simpler to budget for medical costs when there are fixed interest rates and monthly payments.

3. How to Pay for Medical Expenses with a Personal Loan

To use a personal loan to pay for medical expenditures, take these actions:

- **Analyze Your Medical Costs:** Find the total amount required for your hospital bills. Add all expected expenses, including treatments, prescription drugs, and aftercare.

- Compare offers from several lenders to examine your options for a personal loan, paying particular attention to conditions, fees, and interest rates.

- **Apply for the Loan:** Fill out the loan application and send in the necessary supporting documents. To bolster your application, include details regarding your medical costs.

- **Receive Funds:** After the Loan is approved, your bank account will be credited. Use the money to pay for associated costs and medical bills.

- **Manage Your Loan:** Pay consistently to prevent fines and preserve your credit.

Large Purchases

Personal loans can be a great choice for financing large expenditures that you might need help making upfront. This covers everything from financing a dream wedding or trip to purchasing a car.

1. Major Purchase Types

One can utilize personal loans to pay for many different kinds of significant expenditures, such as:

- **Automobiles:** Purchasing a leisure vehicle, motorbike, or new or used automobile.

- **Vacations:** paying for a pricey trip that includes lodging, airfare, and activities.

- **Weddings:** paying for the location, catering, clothes, and entertainment at the wedding.

- Buying significant appliances for the home, such as air conditioning units, washers, dryers, and refrigerators,

- **Electronics:** Purchasing expensive devices like laptops, home entertainment systems, or cell phones.

2. Advantages of Taking Out a Personal Loan to Make Large Purchases

- **Quick Access to Money:** Personal loans give borrowers the money to start big purchases immediately.

- **No Collateral Needed:** Personal loans do not require collateral, which lowers the borrower's risk compared to mortgages or auto loans.

- **Flexible Repayment Terms:** Flexible repayment terms for personal loans allow you to select a repayment plan that works with your budget.

- **Fixed Interest Rates:** Fixed interest rates allow you to manage your money better because they offer consistent monthly payments.

3. How to Use a Personal Loan for Major Purchase Financing

To use a personal loan to pay for a significant purchase, take these actions:

- **Establish Your Budget:** Determine the overall cost of your big buy and ensure it stays within your spending limit.

- **Compare Loan Offers** Loan for the best conditions and interest rates on personal loans. Consider both offline and internet lenders.

- **Please apply for the Loan:** Fill out the loan application and send it in with the required paperwork. Be open and honest about the intention behind the loan.

- **Receive monies:** Once the Loan has been approved, the loan monies will be deposited into your bank account. Spend the money on your significant purchase.

- **Handle Your Loan:** Make your loan installments on time to avoid late fees and keep your credit score high.

Education Costs

Although costly, education is a crucial investment in your future. Personal loans can help defray the cost of education by offering money for books, tuition, and other educational expenditures.

1. Typical Educational Costs Paid for by Personal Loans

You can use personal loans to pay for a range of education-related costs, such as the price of enrolling in classes or programs, which is known as the tuition fee.

- **Books and Supplies:** Investing in study aids, textbooks, and school supplies.
- Purchasing software, a computer, and other essential gear.
- Living expenses include food, rent, and transportation while enrolled in classes.
- **Professional development:** paying for workshops, certificates, or ongoing education courses.

2. Advantages of Taking Out a Personal Loan to Pay for Schooling

- **Fast Funds Access:** With a personal loan, you can get the money you need to pay for schooling.

- **No Collateral Required:** Since personal loans do not need collateral, the borrower bears less risk.

- **Flexible Use:** The funds are available for educational expenses, giving cost management options.

- Monthly installments and fixed interest rates facilitate budgeting for educational costs.

3. How to Pay for Education with a Personal Loan

To use a personal loan to pay for educational expenditures, take these actions:

- **Compute Your Education Costs**: Establish the total amount required to pay for your living expenses, books, and tuition.

- When conducting research on loan options, examine personal loan offers from several lenders and compare terms, fees, and interest rates.

- **Please apply for the Loan:** Fill out the loan application and send it in with the required paperwork. To bolster your application, include information on the costs of your schooling.

- **Receive Funds:** After the Loan is approved, your bank account will be credited. Spend the money on educational expenses.

- **Manage Your Loan:** Make consistent payments to prevent late fines and preserve credit.

Business Outlays

Personal loans are valuable for small business owners and entrepreneurs to cover business-related needs, including launch fees and expansion ambitions. Personal loans offer a flexible funding option when conventional business loans are unavailable.

1. Kinds of Business Expenses That Personal Loans Cover

One can utilize personal loans to pay for a variety of business costs, such as:

- Startup costs include out-of-pocket costs associated with starting a new company, such as supplies, stock, and advertising.

- Funds for paying for regular operating costs like electricity, rent, and wages are known as working capital.

- Expenses related to expanding your company, including setting up shop in a new location or bringing on additional goods or services.

- **Purchase of Equipment:** Purchasing or updating technology and equipment for businesses.

- **Emergency Funds:** For unforeseen costs or shortfalls in cash flow.

2. Advantages of Paying for Business Expenses with a Personal Loan

- **Fast Fund Access:** A personal loan provides immediate access to the money you need to pay for business expenses.

- **No Collateral Needed:** Personal loans, unlike conventional business loans, do not require collateral, which lowers the borrower's risk.

- **Flexible Use:** The money can be used for any business-related activity, giving you more freedom to control your spending.

- Monthly payments and fixed interest rates facilitate the creation of a budget for business spending.

3. How to Pay for Business Expenses with a Personal Loan

To use a personal loan to pay for business expenses, take these actions:

- **Establish Your Business Needs:** Calculate the money you will need for your business's outlays, such as working capital, expansion goals, and launch charges.

- When conducting research on loan options, examine personal loan offers from several lenders and compare terms, fees, and interest rates.

- **Please apply for the Loan:** Fill out the loan application and send it in with the required paperwork. To bolster your application, include information regarding your business expenses.

- **Receive Funds:** The loan amount will be credited to your bank account after approval. Spend the money on expenses associated with your business.

- **Manage Your Loan:** Make consistent payments to prevent late fines and preserve credit.

Unique Occasions

Weddings, significant birthday celebrations, and family reunions are expensive but priceless. Personal loans can give you the money you need to have life-changing experiences without breaking the bank.

1. Different Kinds of Special Events

One can utilize personal loans to fund a range of exceptional occasions, such as:

- **Weddings:** paying for location, food, outfits, entertainment, and photographs.
- Funding birthday festivities or parties for essential anniversaries, such as turning 30, 40, or 50,
- **Family Reunions:** This includes paying for travel, lodging, activities, and other expenses related to planning and hosting a family reunion.
- **Anniversary Celebrations:** paying for excursions or anniversary events commemorating significant marital anniversaries.

2. Advantages of Taking Out a Personal Loan for Unique Occasions

- **Quick Access to Funds:** Personal loans give you the money you need to organize and carry out exceptional occasions quickly.

- **No Collateral Needed:** Personal loans do not require collateral, lowering the borrower's risk compared to other financing options.

- **Flexible Use:** The money is available for any event-related expense, giving cost management options.

- **Fixed Payments:** Budgeting for special occasions is more straightforward, with fixed interest rates and monthly payments.

3. How to Use a Personal Loan to Fund Special Occasions

To use a personal loan to pay for a special occasion, take these actions:

Plan your event: Establish your special event's parameters, including its budget. Make a thorough plan that accounts for all expected costs.

Compare loan Offers: Look for the best conditions and interest rates on personal loans. Consider both offline and internet lenders.

Please apply for the Loan: Fill out the loan application and send it in with the required paperwork. Be open and honest about the intention behind the loan.

Receive monies: Once the loan has been approved, the funds will be deposited into your bank account. Spend the money on event-related costs.

Handle Your Loan: Make your loan installments on time to avoid late fees and keep your credit score high.

Consolidating debt and funding home upgrades are just two uses for personal loans; other uses include paying for large purchases, medical bills, company expenses, education fees, and special occasions. Personal loans are flexible financial instruments. You can make wise selections that support your financial objectives and improve your quality of life by being aware of the many applications for personal loans and knowing how to handle them.

When considering getting a personal loan, it is essential to evaluate offers, comprehend the terms and circumstances, and select a loan that best suits your demands and budget. Whether you want to pay off high-interest debt, make home improvements, save for a big purchase, or pay for unforeseen bills, a personal loan can give you the financial flexibility you need to accomplish your goals.

Chapter Four: Monitoring Credit: Configuring credit surveillance

In the fast-paced world of personal finance, a strong credit score is essential to obtain financial stability and access various financial products. Credit monitoring is a powerful tool that puts you in control, as it continuously tracks your credit activities. By setting up credit monitoring, you empower yourself to stay up-to-date on changes to your credit record, spot inaccuracies, and uncover fraudulent activity. This chapter explains the value of credit monitoring, how to set it up, and how it can help you maintain excellent financial standing.

Comprehending credit monitoring

A credit monitoring service keeps tabs on any modifications to your credit reports from Equifax, Experian, and TransUnion, the three main credit bureaus. It notifies you of any updates that could affect your credit score, such as new accounts, inquiries, public records, or other changes. You can prevent problems and safeguard your financial reputation by closely monitoring your credit.

1. **The Significance of Credit Monitoring**

    - **Pre-fraud Identification:** Credit monitoring enables you to quickly take action to reduce fraud by alerting you to questionable activity, such as new accounts opened in your name or illegal credit queries.

    - **Error Identification:** Inaccuracies in your credit report, like out-of-date or inaccurate account information, can hurt your credit score. Monitoring enables you to identify these mistakes and quickly challenge them.

    - **Credit Score Management:** By receiving regular updates on your credit report, you may better understand the variables that affect your credit score and make decisions that will either strengthen or preserve your credit.

    - **Comfort:** You can rest easy knowing that your credit is being watched. This proactive approach means you won't be as surprised by any bad changes or fraudulent activity, providing security and peace of mind.

2. **Types of credit monitoring services.**

    - Essential credit monitoring usually entails receiving alerts when there are significant changes to your credit report, like opening new accounts, inquiries, or public records.

- Comprehensive Credit Monitoring: Provides more thorough monitoring, including alerts for changes from all three major credit bureaus. It may include other features like credit score tracking and identity theft insurance.
- Credit score monitoring provides frequent updates and insights into the elements influencing your score, primarily focusing on changes to your credit score.

How to establish credit monitoring

Although choosing the best credit monitoring service for your needs is a deliberate process, setting it up is simple. To set up efficient credit monitoring, follow these steps: 1. Assess your requirements. 2. Look into credit monitoring companies. 3. Examine and contrast features and services. 4. Enroll in a credit monitoring program. 5. Keep an eye on and preserve your credit health.

1. Assess your requirements.

Consider your financial and personal needs before choosing a credit monitoring service. Take into account the following elements:

- **Monitoring Level:** Assess your needs to see if you require simple monitoring or more extensive coverage, such as credit score tracking and identity theft protection.

- **Budget:** Determine the maximum amount you can pay for credit monitoring services. While some programs offer advanced features for a monthly or annual cost, others are free.

- **Features:** List the exact features you desire, such as access to credit scores from all three main bureaus, comprehensive credit reports, identity theft insurance, and real-time notifications.

2. Look into credit monitoring companies.

After determining what you need, compare credit monitoring companies to see which best suits your needs. Several renowned suppliers consist of:

- **Credit bureaus:** Equifax, Experian, and TransUnion each have a credit monitoring service.

- **Providers that work with third parties,** such as Credit Karma, Identity Guard, and myFICO, are just a few of the businesses that offer complete credit monitoring services.

- **Financial Institutions:** Several credit unions and banks provide credit monitoring services to their clientele, frequently at a reduced cost or as a component of a larger economic package.

3. Examine and contrast features and services.

When comparing credit monitoring services, consider the following factors:

- **Coverage:** To ensure thorough protection, make sure the service keeps an eye on all three major credit bureaus.
- **Alerts:** Look for services that send real-time or almost real-time alerts for changes to your credit report.
- **Reports and Scores:** Determine the frequency of updates and whether the service gives you regular access to your credit reports and scores.
- **Protection Against Identity Theft:** Consider extra features like fraud resolution support, dark web surveillance, and identity theft insurance.
- **Experience of the User:** Examine user evaluations and comments to determine how dependable and user-friendly the service is.

User experience is a crucial factor to consider when choosing a credit monitoring service. Look for services that have positive user reviews and provide excellent customer support.

4. Enroll in a credit monitoring program.

Once you have decided on a credit monitoring service, register by doing the following:

- **Establish an Account:** Go to the provider's website and register by entering your contact information, name, address, Social Security number, and other personal data.

- **Check Your Identity:** Finish the verification procedure, which could entail utilizing multi-factor authentication, submitting identity papers, or responding to security questions.

- **Choose a scheme:** Select a monitoring plan based on your needs and financial constraints. While some companies have tiered plans with diffcrent levels of coverage and functionality, others offer free essential monitoring.

- **Configure Notifications:** Set up your alert settings to receive text, email, or mobile app notifications. Establish alert thresholds for things like new account openings or credit score changes.

- **Examine your credit reports:** After enrolling, familiarize yourself with the tracked data by reviewing your credit reports. Make a note of any disparities or strange accounts that require attention.

5. Keep an eye on and preserve your credit health.

Manage and preserve your credit health after you have set up credit monitoring:

- **Quickly React to Alerts:** Take immediate action upon receiving an alert regarding modifications to your credit report. Look into the reason and take appropriate action, such as filing a fraud report or contesting mistakes.

- **Examine Credit Reports Frequently:** You should routinely check the accuracy and thoroughness of your credit reports, even if you are using credit monitoring.

- **Develop Reputable Credit Habits:** By making on-time bill payments, limiting credit card balances, avoiding pointless credit queries, and handling debt sensibly, you may preserve a good credit score.

Advantages of Credit Monitoring

Several advantages to credit monitoring can significantly improve your financial security and well-being. Here are a few main benefits:

1. Early Fraudulent Activity Detection

Early fraud identification is one of the most essential advantages of credit monitoring. You will get alerts if someone tries to make illicit purchases or start a new credit account in your name. This early identification not only enables you to dispute fraudulent charges, freeze your credit, and inform law enforcement, but also makes you feel protected and secure.

2. Identity Theft Prevention

Features like identity theft insurance and dark web monitoring are standard inclusions in credit monitoring services. By warning you of questionable activity and offering financial protection if your identity is stolen, these features aid in preventing identity theft.

3. Precise Credit Reporting

You can make sure that your credit reports are accurate and current by regularly reviewing them. You may keep a higher credit score and prevent potential adverse effects on your creditworthiness by quickly recognizing and disputing inaccuracies.

4. Goal-setting and financial planning

You can monitor your credit development over time by accessing regular credit reports and scores. You may use this information to organize your finances better and create goals because it clarifies how your credit actions affect your score and how you can raise it.

5. Better Credit Card and Loan Offers

Better loan and credit card offers with cheaper interest rates and better terms can result from having a high credit score. Keeping an eye on your credit report and score high will allow you to seize these chances when they present themselves.

Credit monitoring is crucial to safeguard your financial well-being and accomplish your financial objectives. You can ensure the accuracy of your credit information, stay up-to-date on changes to your credit report, and catch fraud early by setting up credit monitoring. Setting up credit monitoring entails assessing your requirements, investigating potential providers, contrasting plans, and keeping a close eye on the state of your credit.

With the correct credit monitoring service, having your credit under observation and focusing on creating a safe financial future may be yours. Credit monitoring offers the supervision and assistance you require to succeed, whether your goals are to raise your credit score, prevent identity theft, or keep track of your financial situation.

Notifications and Alerts for Credit Monitoring

Protecting your financial health is more important than ever in the digital era. To be informed about any changes or possible problems, credit monitoring is a crucial tool that assists you in keeping tabs on your credit reports and ratings. Notifications and alerts are among the most critical aspects of credit monitoring services. These regular updates give you up-to-date knowledge about essential modifications to your credit profile, allowing you to respond quickly if needed. This chapter explores the value of alerts and notifications, their operation, the many kinds of alerts, and how you may use them to keep your credit score in good standing.

The Significance of Warnings and Alerts

The main components of credit monitoring services are notifications and alerts. They serve as an early warning system, enabling you to monitor your credit activity and respond quickly if necessary. Alerts and notifications are essential for the following principal reasons:

1. Detection of fraud early on

Early detection of fraudulent activity is one of the main advantages of credit monitoring notifications.

You will get alerts if someone tries to make unlawful transactions or start a new account in your name. Early discovery enables you to take quick action to lessen the harm, including getting in touch with the creditor, freezing your credit, and reporting the incident to the Federal Trade Commission (FTC).

2. Identification of Errors

Credit reports can show errors such as obsolete addresses, misreported payments, or inaccurate account information. You can immediately detect these mistakes with alerts and notifications, allowing you to contest the errors with the credit bureaus and resolving mistakes as soon as possible guarantees that your credit report fairly portrays your financial background, which is necessary to keep your credit score high.

3. Management of Credit Scores

You can better understand the variables affecting your credit health by receiving regular updates regarding modifications to your credit report and score. Receiving alerts regarding account balance adjustments, new accounts, and credit queries will help you make wise decisions that will raise or preserve your credit score. By being proactive, you can take charge of your financial destiny.

4. Mental peace

It gives you comfort to know that your credit is being watched. Thanks to alerts and notifications, you no longer need to perform manual credit checks to be informed about your credit status. This automated oversight lessens the stress of managing your credit by guaranteeing you are always informed of critical changes.

How Notifications and Alerts Operate

Credit monitoring services offer alerts and notifications Through various platforms, such as email, SMS, and mobile apps. The program will automatically notify you whenever there is a substantial update to your credit report. This is how the procedure operates typically:

1. Information Gathering

Credit monitoring services obtain information continuously from Equifax, Experian, and TransUnion, the three leading credit agencies. This data comprises queries, public records, payment history, and credit account information.

2. Change Recognition

The program looks for notable changes in your credit report using advanced algorithms. These modifications may involve establishing a new account, making hard inquiries, adjusting account balances, making late payments, or creating new public records like tax liens or bankruptcies.

3. Warning Production

The service sends out an alert if it finds a significant change. The notification contains information regarding the modification, including the kind of account impacted, when it was made, and, if relevant, how it will affect your credit score.

4. Delivery of Notifications

Afterwards, you receive the alert by email, SMS, or mobile app notification you selected. Customizing your alert options allows you to receive messages for particular updates or at predetermined thresholds from certain providers.

5. User Initiation

After receiving an alert, you can review the information and take the necessary action. This could be getting in touch with the creditor to confirm the creation of an account, disputing a mistake with the credit agency, or making efforts to raise your credit score.

Credit Monitoring Alert Types

Credit monitoring services provide many alerts to keep you updated on various elements of your credit profile. You can get the most out of your credit monitoring service by knowing the different notifications. These are a few examples of typical credit monitoring alert types:

1. Alerts for New Accounts

You can receive notifications via new account alerts whenever someone opens a new credit account in your name. Credit cards, loans, mortgages, and other credit lines fall into this category. This notice may indicate possible fraud if you did not apply for the account.

2. Alerts for Credit Inquiry

When a lender or creditor looks up your credit record to determine your creditworthiness, this is a credit inquiry. Alerts about hard inquiries on your credit report let you know when they happen. It is critical to keep a close eye on them since several hard inquiries in a short time can negatively affect your credit score.

3. Alerts for Account Balance

Account balance alerts let you know when there are any notable adjustments to the amounts on your current credit accounts. This may involve changes to the amounts owed on your loans, credit card debt, or other credit lines. Keeping an eye on your account balances will assist you in controlling your credit usage ratio, an essential component of your credit score.

4. Notifications of Late Payment

When a payment appears on your credit record as late, you will receive a notification about it. Getting timely notices enables you to take prompt action, such as disputing the late payment with the creditor or making the payment, as late payments can negatively affect your credit score.

5. Alerts for Public Records

When new public records, such as judgments, tax liens, or bankruptcies, are posted to your credit report, public record notifications let you know about them. It is critical to be aware of these records and, if necessary, take proper action, as they can seriously harm your credit score.

6. Alerts for Credit Score Changes

When your credit score significantly changes, credit score change alerts let you know. Numerous things, including creating new accounts, credit inquiries, account balance adjustments, and late payments, maybe the cause. You can better manage your credit by being aware of the factors that affect your credit score.

7. Alerts for Identity Theft

Identity theft alerts are a feature of several credit monitoring services that inform you about any questionable activity that might point to identity theft. Alerts for alterations to your address or Social Security number and notifications for newly opened accounts in your name are examples of this.

Advantages of Notifications and Alerts

Notifications and alerts from credit monitoring services have many advantages that can significantly improve your financial health. Here are a few main benefits:

1. Preventing fraud proactively

If you get warnings about new accounts or credit queries, you can immediately identify any fraud and stop the damage. By taking preventative measures, you can lessen the effects of identity theft and safeguard your credit.

2. Better Credit Administration

You may monitor your credit health by receiving regular notifications regarding modifications to your credit report and score. You can maintain or raise your credit score by checking your account balances, payment history, and credit inquiries. This will help you make wise decisions.

3. Prompt error correction

Credit monitoring notifications can assist you in swiftly locating mistakes on your credit report. You can ensure that your credit report accurately portrays your financial history by raising any inaccuracies as soon as you notice them. Having a decent credit score depends on this.

4. Improved Budgetary Scheduling

Access to frequent credit updates lets you monitor your credit's development over time. You may use this information to organize your finances better and create goals because it clarifies how your credit actions affect your score and how you can raise it.

5. Mental steadiness

It gives you comfort to know that your credit is being watched. Thanks to alerts and notifications, you no longer need to perform manual credit checks to be informed about your credit status. This automated oversight lessens the stress of managing your credit by guaranteeing you are always informed of significant changes.

Selecting the Best Monitoring Service for Credit

Given the abundance of options available, selecting the best credit monitoring service might take time.

When choosing a credit monitoring service, take into account the following factors:

1. Protection

Ensure the service monitors Equifax, Experian, and TransUnion, the leading credit agencies. Comprehensive coverage ensures you receive real-time updates from all credit bureaus and gives you a comprehensive picture of your credit history.

2. Types of Alerts

Choose a service that provides a variety of alerts, such as alerts for new accounts, credit inquiries, account balances, late payments, changes to credit scores, public record alerts, and identity theft alerts. You will be better protected if the alarm system is more extensive.

3. Update Frequency

Think about how often the service delivers alerts and changes your credit information. While some services update less frequently, others may provide real-time or almost real-time notifications. For credit monitoring to be effective, timely updates are essential.

4. Extra Features

Examine the business's extra features, like credit score tracking, dark web monitoring, identity theft protection, and access to comprehensive credit reports. These additional security layers and features can increase the value of the credit monitoring service.

5. Price

Examine the prices of several credit monitoring programs. A monthly or annual subscription fee is required for certain services; however, they are all paid. Evaluate each service's features and benefits to see if the price is reasonable.

6. Experience of the User

Examine user evaluations and comments to determine how dependable and user-friendly the service is. A good credit monitoring experience requires an intuitive user interface and prompt customer service.

Putting notifications and alerts in place

It is simple to set up alerts and notifications with the credit monitoring service of your choice. The general procedures are as follows:

1. Register for an Account

Go to the provider's website and document by entering your contact information, name, address, Social Security number, and other personal data.

2. Confirm your identity.

Finish the identity verification procedure, which could entail utilizing multi-factor authentication, submitting identity papers, or responding to security questions.

3. Adjust the preferencespreferences for alerts.

Establish your alert preferences by deciding which alert categories and channels (email, SMS, or mobile app notifications) you would like to receive. Adjust the alert thresholds to meet your requirements.

4. Examine and verify

Verify your selections and review your alert settings. To ensure you receive notifications on time, ensure your contact information is correct and current.

5. Keep an eye on things and react.

After configuring your alerts and notifications, keep a close eye on your credit and swiftly respond to any alerts. Examine the specifics of every warning and take the necessary steps, like confirming new accounts, raising concerns about mistakes, or addressing overdue payments.

A vital part of credit monitoring services is alerts and notifications, which give you up-to-date information in real-time regarding important alterations to your credit profile. You may successfully manage your credit score, uncover inaccuracies, spot fraud early, and stay updated about your credit activity by setting up and personalizing notifications. Proactive fraud protection, better credit management, prompt error correction, improved financial planning, and peace of mind are some advantages of receiving credit monitoring notifications.

Evaluating characteristics, including coverage, alert types, update frequency, extra features, cost, and user experience, are all important when selecting the best credit monitoring service. Upon choosing a service, configuring alerts and notifications is a simple procedure that guarantees you always stay informed about significant alterations to your credit report.

You may confidently reach your financial objectives and take charge of your financial well-being by utilizing the power of credit monitoring alerts and notifications.

Protection Against Theft of Identity

Identity theft has become a familiar and significant threat to people's financial security in our increasingly digital environment. Identity theft can have disastrous repercussions, from severely low credit ratings to substantial monetary losses. Credit monitoring, which continuously monitors your credit activity and notifies you of any odd changes, is an effective weapon in the fight against identity theft. This chapter covers various topics related to preventing identity theft, such as knowing how identity theft happens, how credit monitoring can help, what to do if you become a victim, and proactive ways to protect your personal data.

Comprehending Identity Theft

Understanding Identity Theft: The more you know about identity theft, the more empowered you are to protect yourself. Identity theft is the act of someone using your personal information to perpetrate fraud or other crimes without your consent. This data may contain your name, Social Security number, and credit card number. Thieves can use this information to apply for loans, create new credit accounts, make purchases they should not have, and even commit crimes under your name.

Identity Theft Types

Numerous varieties of identity theft exist, each with a unique set of hazards and repercussions. Knowing the various forms of identity theft will enable you to identify any dangers and take the necessary precautions to keep yourself safe.

The most prevalent kind of identity theft is financial identity theft, in which criminals use your data to access your bank accounts, apply for new credit cards, apply for loans, or make unapproved transactions.

Tax Identity Theft: When someone files false tax returns and requests reimbursements in your name, they might use your Social Security number as leverage. This may result in issues with the IRS and considerable delays in getting your rightful tax refund.

Medical Identity Theft: In this type of theft, thieves steal your personal information to make false insurance claims, buy prescription medications, or get medical attention. Inaccurate entries in your medical records and changes to your insurance coverage may result from this.

Theft of criminal identities: If thieves get you arrested and give your information to the police, they might utilize your personal information. Legal issues and a criminal record in your name may arise from this.

Employment Identity Theft: Thieves utilize personal information, such as your Social Security number, to apply for jobs. It may result in problems for you in terms of taxes and Social Security benefits.

Theft of synthetic identities involves thieves creating a false identity by fusing authentic and fraudulent information, which they then use to open accounts and commit fraud. It is challenging to identify and stop this kind of theft.

Credit Monitoring's Function in Preventing Identity Theft

Because credit monitoring keeps a close eye on your credit activities, it is essential for preventing identity theft. It facilitates the early detection of questionable activity, enabling you to respond quickly to minimize possible harm. The following are some ways that credit monitoring can guard against identity theft:

1. Alerts in Real Time

Credit monitoring services offer real-time alerts when there are significant changes to your credit report, such as new public records, account openings, credit queries, account balance adjustments, or changes in credit. With the help of these notifications, you may quickly identify any unauthorized activity and take the appropriate action to stop additional harm.

2. Extensive Coverage

Credit monitoring services frequently keep tabs on your credit transactions at Equifax, Experian, and TransUnion, the three leading credit agencies. Comprehensive coverage gives you a thorough picture of your credit activity and potential threats by keeping you informed of any changes from any bureau.

3. Features to Prevent Identity Theft

Identity theft insurance, fraud resolution support, and dark web monitoring are just a few of the extra identity theft protection options many credit monitoring services provide. These features improve your capacity to safeguard your private data and, in the unlikely event of identity theft, to recover from it.

4. Frequent Credit Scores and Reports

Regular access to credit reports and scores enables you to keep an eye on the state of your credit and identify any irregularities or questionable activity. Regularly checking your credit reports lessens the impact of identity theft by assisting you in spotting mistakes and unlawful activity early on.

5. Learning and Materials

Credit monitoring services frequently include instructional materials and instruments to assist you in identifying possible risks, comprehending identity theft, and taking preventative action to safeguard your data. With the help of these materials, you can protect your financial stability and make wise judgments.

Actions to Take in the Event of Identity Theft

Actions to Take in the Event of Identity Theft: Even with the best intentions, identity theft can still occur. However, taking immediate action can significantly reduce harm and start recovery. If you believe you have been the victim of identity theft, the following actions are necessary:

1. Update Your Credit Reports with a Fraud Alert

To add a fraud alert to your credit reports, contact Equifax, Experian, or TransUnion, the three leading credit agencies. A fraud warning alerts creditors to the possibility that you are a victim of identity theft and advises them to take further precautions to confirm your identity before granting credit. When you file a fraud alert, one of the bureaus will alert the other two.

2. Examine your credit reports

Get complimentary copies of your credit reports from the three leading credit reporting agencies, and thoroughly check them for unauthorized activities, inquiries, or accounts. Examine the data for errors and unusual entries, and note any questionable activity.

3. Put Your Credit on Hold

Think about freezing the credit on your credit reports. A credit freeze makes it more difficult for identity thieves to open new accounts in your name by limiting access to your credit reports. You must contact each credit bureau directly to put a freeze in place and remove it later if needed.

4. File an Identity Theft Report

Report a theft online at IdentityTheft.gov to the Federal Trade Commission (FTC). To contest false accounts and activity, the FTC will give you an Identity Theft Report and a recovery plan customized to your circumstances.

5. Speak with Your Financial Providers

Inform your credit card providers, banks, and other lenders of the identity theft. Request new card and account numbers, then close or freeze any compromised accounts. Keep a careful eye on your accounts to spot any fraudulent activity.

6. Contest False Charges and Accounts

Contact the creditors and companies that formed the bogus accounts or made the unlawful charges. Tell them about the identity theft, ask them to cancel the accounts, and have any bogus charges removed. Please give them your identity theft report and any additional supporting files.

7. Make a Police Report

Make a report to the police department in your community. Please give them your identity theft report and any further proof you have of the theft. If you need to prove your identity or contest fraudulent activity, a police report can be helpful.

8. Keep an eye on your accounts and credit

Look for any new questionable activity in your financial accounts and credit reports. Consider signing up for a credit monitoring program that includes identity theft protection features for assistance and real-time notifications during the recovery process.

Preventive Steps to Safeguard Your Data

The best line of protection against identity theft is prevention. You may lessen your chances of being a victim by proactively protecting your personal information. You can take the following actions to protect your personal information:

1. Protect Your Private Records

Store all your documents safely, including your birth certificate, Social Security card, and bank statements. When discarding documents that include personal information, shred any sensitive documents you are not taking with you.

2. Make Use of Security Measures and Strong Passwords

Ensure your online accounts have secure, one-of-a-kind passwords that you update frequently. To make your password difficult to guess, use a combination of letters, numbers, and special characters instead of things like your name or birthdate. To increase security, turn on multi-factor authentication (MFA).

3. Keep an eye on your financial statements

Ensure there have been no fraudulent transactions by routinely checking your credit card, bank, and other financial account statements. Notify your financial institution right once if you witness any questionable activity.

4. Exercise Caution While Sharing Personal Info Online

Take care while sharing information online, especially on social media. Do not share private information online, such as your name, address, or birthdate. To manage who can view your information, use your privacy settings. It would help to exercise caution when accepting friend requests from someone you do not know.

5. Keep Your Electronics Safe

Antivirus software, firewalls, and routine software upgrades can help you safeguard your PCs, smartphones, and other gadgets. When using public Wi-Fi networks for financial transactions, use caution and use encryption to protect confidential information.

6. Identify Phishing Schemes

Be cautious when responding to unwanted calls, emails, or messages that request personal information. Phishing scammers frequently pose as reputable companies to fool you into divulging personal information. Check the legitimacy of any inquiries by contacting the company directly using its official contact details.

7. Restrict Who Can Access Your Data

Share your personal information only with people and organizations you can trust. Exercise caution when disclosing your Social Security number, bank account number, and other private information.

8. Employ Services to Prevent Identity Theft

Consider signing up for a service that protects against identity theft and provides services like fraud support, insurance against identity theft, and monitoring of the dark web. These services offer extra security and assistance if you fall prey to identity theft.

Overview

Identity theft is a severe and expanding risk that can seriously harm financial stability. Credit monitoring, which continuously monitors your credit activity and notifies you of any odd changes, is an effective weapon in the fight against identity theft. You may significantly lower your chance of being a victim by being aware of the many forms of identity theft, using credit monitoring services, and taking preventative steps to safeguard your data.

In the unlikely event that identity theft occurs to you, it is imperative that you take immediate action, minimize damage, and start the healing process. Essential steps to take include:

- Setting up fraud alerts.
- Freezing your credit.
- Reporting the theft to the proper authorities.
- Keep a careful eye on your accounts.

You can guard against identity theft and guarantee the security of your finances by being watchful and knowledgeable. Remember that prevention is always the best defence, and you can protect your private data and feel secure in an increasingly digital environment by using the appropriate tools and techniques.

Chapter 5: Suggestions for Financial Products

It can be overwhelming to navigate the complex world of financial products. With so many options available, it's challenging to determine which products best suit your unique financial needs and goals. The purpose of personalized product recommendations is to alleviate this pressure by using technology and data to provide tailored suggestions. This chapter delves into the value, operation, and benefits of personalized financial product recommendations. We will also explore specific product categories, such as insurance, mortgages, and credit cards, and demonstrate how personalized recommendations can help you make informed decisions in each area, relieving you of the stress of making these choices alone.

The Significance of Tailored Financial Product Suggestions

In the current fast-paced financial market, recommendations for personalized financial products have grown in value. They provide several significant benefits that assist customers in making wiser financial decisions.

Relevance: Personalized recommendations ensure that the items are relevant to your needs by considering your unique financial condition, preferences, and ambitions.

Efficiency: Personalized recommendations save you time and effort when researching and comparing financial products. By narrowing down the wide range of options to those that best match your profile, they allow you to make decisions more quickly and with less effort, making you feel more efficient.

Making Informed Decisions: Accessing personalized recommendations provides you with the knowledge to choose products that align with your financial goals. This empowerment can boost your confidence in your financial decisions.

Improved Results: Based on your situation, personalized product recommendations can help you find products that provide the best terms, rates, and advantages. This can result in improved financial outcomes.

How Customized Product Recommendations Operate

How Customized Product Recommendations Work using advanced algorithms, data analytics, and machine learning, personalized product recommendations evaluate your financial situation and preferences. Here's a detailed breakdown of the typical process:

Data collection: Gathering information about your financial status, such as your income, spending, credit score, current debts, financial objectives, and preferences, is the first phase in the process. This data can be acquired through online forms, smartphone apps, or direct interaction with your financial accounts.

Profile Analysis: After gathering the information, complex algorithms examine your financial profile to find trends, patterns, and essential metrics. This study evaluates your financial needs and objectives and assists in determining your eligibility for different financial solutions.

Product Matching: The system connects you with financial goods that best fit your profile based on the analysis. The matching process ensures the suggested products meet your financial goals by considering variables like interest rates, fees, rewards, bonuses, and periods.

Suggestions: The algorithm creates customized product recommendations after providing a well-chosen range of possibilities. To help you make an informed choice, each recommendation contains comprehensive information about the product, including its features, benefits, and pitfalls.

Continuous Monitoring and Optimization: Systems that recommend personalized products frequently involve constant monitoring and optimization. The system ensures you always have access to the most relevant and advantageous items by updating its suggestions to reflect changes in your financial status and ambitions.

Customized Credit Card Product Recommendations

Credit cards are a popular kind of financial equipment that provides rewards, ease, and the opportunity to establish credit. Finding the ideal credit card can be difficult because so many possibilities are available. You may find credit cards that best fit your spending patterns, credit score, and financial objectives with personalized product recommendations.

Rewards on Various Credit Card Types Credit cards: These cards provide cashback, points, or miles for transactions. Personalized recommendations can assist you in selecting a rewards card that best suits your spending patterns and maximizes the points you accrue from regular transactions.

Credit Cards with a Low or 0% initial APR for Balance Transfers: A balance transfer card can help you save money on interest payments if you already have credit card debt. Based on your credit profile, personalized recommendations might help you find balance transfer cards with good terms.

Travel credit cards: Made for those who travel frequently, these cards come with incentives and perks like hotel points, airline miles, and travel insurance. You can find a travel card that fits your travel habits and tastes with personalized suggestions.

Secured Credit Cards: Secured credit cards assist in establishing or restoring credit and are suitable for people with little or no credit history. However, they do demand a security deposit. Using personalized suggestions, you can choose secured cards with the most significant terms and perks according to your circumstances.

Low-Interest Credit Cards: These cards are perfect for people who might have a balance because they have lower ongoing interest rates. You may select low-interest cards that fit your credit profile and financial objectives with the aid of personalized recommendations.

Personalized Credit Card Recommendations' Advantages

Optimized Gains and Incentives: Personalized suggestions ensure you choose a credit card with features and incentives that match your spending patterns, enabling you to get the most out of your card.

Cost savings: Personalized recommendations can help you reduce the amount you pay in fees and interest by finding credit cards with advantageous terms, interest rates, and fees.

Enhanced Credit Score: Over time, you can raise your credit score by choosing the best credit card and using it responsibly. Personalized suggestions might match you with cards that report to the major credit agencies and offer features to help you manage your credit.

Convenience: By streamlining the selection process, personalized credit card recommendations help you locate the ideal card faster and with less effort.

Personalized Mortgage Product Recommendations

Achieving your ambitions of becoming a homeowner requires a significant financial commitment, so choosing the correct mortgage program is essential. Personalized mortgage suggestions will assist you in navigating the complicated mortgage market and determining which options are ideal for you in light of your goals for homeownership and financial situation.

Mortgage Types

Fixed-rate mortgages: These mortgages provide predictable monthly payments and have a fixed interest rate for the duration of the loan. You can locate fixed-rate mortgages with reasonable rates and terms and personalized recommendations.

Mortgages with adjustable rates (ARMs) provide a fixed interest rate for a predetermined amount of time, after which it will fluctuate based on market rates regularly. Customized recommendations can help find ARMs with reasonable starting rates and adjustment terms.

- **FHA Loans:** Guaranteed by the Federal Housing Administration (FHA), these loans are intended for borrowers with weaker credit ratings and first-time homebuyers. With tailored recommendations, you can locate FHA loans that fit your requirements and credentials.

- **VA Loans:** Offering attractive terms and no down payment requirements, VA loans are accessible to qualified veterans and active-duty military personnel. With tailored recommendations, you can locate VA loans with the best perks for your circumstances.

- **Jumbo Loans:** These loans provide higher loan amounts than conforming loan limitations for properties of high value. You can locate jumbo loans with competitive rates and conditions and personalized recommendations.

- **Refinance Mortgages:** Refinancing your mortgage might help you access home equity, get a cheaper interest rate, or cut monthly payments. Personalized recommendations can help find refinance solutions with the most benefits and savings.

Personalized Mortgage Recommendations' Advantages

- **Reduced Interest Rates:** Based on your credit history and financial circumstances, personalized recommendations can assist you in locating mortgage products with the lowest interest rates, saving you money over the loan.

- **Personalized Loan Terms:** We ensure that your loan terms align with your financial goals and aspirations to become a homeowner by matching you with mortgage products that offer advantageous terms.

- **Enhanced Prospects of Approval:** Tailored mortgage suggestions consider your financial background and eligibility, assisting you in determining which products have the highest probability of approval.

- **Cost Savings:** Personalized recommendations can help you save money on closing costs and other expenses by highlighting mortgage packages with reduced fees and advantageous conditions.

- **Simplified Process:** Personalized mortgage suggestions streamline choosing the ideal mortgage by saving you time and effort when investigating and comparing choices.

Personalized Insurance Product Recommendations

Insurance is vital to financial planning since it offers security and assurance for various life situations. Whether you are searching for life, health, vehicle, or house insurance, personalized insurance suggestions will assist you in finding the best plans to suit your needs.

Insurance Types

- Health Insurance: Prescription drugs, hospital stays, and doctor visits are healthcare costs that health insurance helps pay for. Based on your healthcare demands and financial situation, personalized recommendations can assist you in locating health insurance plans with the best coverage and perks.

- Auto Insurance: This type of insurance shields you financially from mishaps with your car, including theft and accidents. Personalized recommendations can help you find auto insurance plans with the best discounts and coverage for your car and driving style.

- Homeowners insurance shields your house and belongings from harm, theft, and legal responsibility. You can select policies with personalized recommendations that provide benefits and comprehensive coverage for your home and possessions.

- Renters Insurance: For people renting out their houses, renters insurance offers liability and personal property protection. Personalized recommendations can help you find renters insurance plans with the best benefits and coverage.

- Life Insurance: In the case of your passing, life insurance protects your loved ones financially. Based on your financial objectives and family situation, personalized advice can assist you in locating life insurance products that provide the appropriate coverage and benefits.

- Disability Insurance: If a sickness or injury prevents you from working, disability insurance replaces your lost income. Based on your work and financial demands, personalized recommendations will assist you in locating disability insurance policies that provide the best coverage and benefits.

- Long-Term Care Insurance: This type of insurance pays for the expenses of providing long-term care services, including in-home and nursing home care. Based on your health and financial circumstances, personalized recommendations can assist you in locating insurance that offers the best coverage and benefits.

Personalized Insurance Recommendations' Advantages

- Customized Coverage: Personalized advice ensures you choose insurance plans that give the appropriate coverage for your situation, giving you financial security and peace of mind.

- Cost Savings: Personalized recommendations can help you reduce the cost of your insurance by pointing out insurance plans with affordable rates and discounts.

- Enhanced Protection: Customized insurance suggestions consider your unique risks and coverage requirements to ensure you are adequately safeguarded against any hazards.

- Simplified Process: By reducing the time and effort required for options research and comparison, personalized insurance recommendations help you locate the best policies.

- Ongoing Optimization: You can always have the most pertinent and advantageous coverage by having personalized suggestions updated as your circumstances and insurance needs change.

With personalized financial product recommendations, you may effectively traverse the complicated world of financial products, improving your ability to make wise decisions and get better financial results. Personalized suggestions make recommendations based on your goals and economic profile, using data and technology to ensure you choose the items that best suit your needs.

Whether you are searching for insurance, mortgages, or credit cards, tailored product recommendations will assist you in finding the deals with the best features, rates, and conditions. By using tailored recommendations, you may make well-informed decisions that promote your financial well-being and health while saving time, effort, and money.

It is essential to consider your long-term financial objectives and closely monitor your finances while investigating proposals for individualized financial products. You can guarantee that you always have access to the most advantageous and pertinent financial goods by being proactive and knowledgeable, enabling you to reach your financial goals confidently.

Chapter 6: An AI-Powered Financial Advisor, Meet Molly

These days, technology permeates every aspect of our lives, and money management is no different. You introduce Molly, the AI-powered financial advisor who will completely change how you handle your money. Molly is more than simply a digital assistant; she is a knowledgeable, proactive, and individualized advisor who gives you the confidence and ease to navigate the complex world of financial planning.

Who is this Molly?

Molly is a cutting-edge artificial intelligence financial advisor designed to offer individualized financial guidance and assistance. She can evaluate your economic activity, spot trends, and provide customized recommendations to help you reach your financial objectives. But what sets her apart is her ability to simplify complex financial decisions, empowering you with the confidence to make the right choices. She does this by using cutting-edge machine learning algorithms and data analytics. Molly is here to help you every step of the way, whether your goals are to save more, make intelligent investments, pay off debt, or manage your daily finances better.

Principal Aspects of Molly's Tailored Financial Advice: Molly provides tailored financial guidance according to your financial circumstances, objectives, and preferences. She gives you concrete advice and ideas that you can put into practice.

Real-Time Data Analysis: Molly can provide the most recent recommendations and plan modifications by continuously evaluating your financial data. This real-time method ensures you have access to the most up-to-date information.

Molly is not just about setting goals; she's about helping you achieve them. She assists you in establishing reasonable financial objectives and monitors your progress toward accomplishing them. She gives you advice and updates frequently to help you stay on course, providing the support and guidance you need to succeed.

Spending Insights: Molly examines your spending habits to find areas where you may make savings and cost reductions. She offers thorough reports and pointers on handling your spending more effectively.

Investment Advice: Molly provides information about investments that fit your risk tolerance and financial objectives. She oversees the performance of your varied portfolio and assists you in building it.

Debt management: Molly offers methods for paying off debt that you already have in a timely and effective manner. She guides debt consolidation, obtaining reduced interest rates, and arranging a payback schedule.

Molly assists you in creating and adhering to a budget that fits your financial goals and way of life. She sends you alerts and reminders to ensure you stick to your spending plan.

Security and Privacy: Molly is built to the strictest security and privacy requirements. She ensures the security of your financial data through robust encryption and other advanced security measures. Your personal information is kept private and secure, giving you peace of mind as you work with Molly to manage your finances.

Tailored Money Advice

Molly's ability to offer individualized financial advice is one of her strongest suits. In contrast to general counsel, Molly's recommendations are customized to your situation, making them extraordinarily pertinent and helpful. Here are some methods Molly provides individualized financial advice:

1. Routines for Daily Spending

Molly monitors your everyday expenses and spots trends that might impact your financial stability. For instance, if she observes high costs associated with eating out, she can advise cooking more regularly at home to save money. She can also recommend particular apps or tools to improve your tracking of expenditures.

2. Money Management Techniques

Molly provides customized saving solutions based on your objectives, spending, and income. If you are saving for a trip, she may recommend a weekly amount to put aside. She can also offer you a thorough strategy for accumulating an emergency fund in a predetermined amount of time.

3. Debt Settlement

Molly can offer you individualized advice on effective debt reduction if you are in debt. She can advise prioritizing high-interest debt, combining loans, or establishing automatic payments to prevent late fees. She can also guide you in bargaining with creditors for better terms.

4. Investment Prospects

Molly evaluates your financial objectives and market developments to recommend appropriate investment alternatives. Molly offers information on possible returns and risks for equities, bonds, and mutual funds, assisting you in making well-informed decisions. To reduce risk, she can also suggest diversifying your holdings.

5. Making Retirement Plans

Retirement planning can be complicated, but Molly makes it easier by offering individualized advice. She determines how much you need to save by considering your present savings and your ideal retirement lifestyle. She also advises on the appropriate investment plans and retirement accounts to help you achieve your objectives.

6. Cost Control

Molly offers targeted cost-cutting advice to help you manage your expenditures. She might suggest refinancing a debt, finding savings on regular subscriptions, or moving to a more reasonably priced utility provider. Her mission is to maximize your financial resources without sacrificing your standard of living.

7. Raising Credit Scores

Your credit score is essential for financial stability. Molly offers advice on how to raise your credit score through responsible credit card use, timely bill payment, and rectification of any inaccuracies on your credit report. She also provides guidance on loans and credit cards suitable for your particular credit profile.

8. Tax Parity

Molly provides tailored advice on maximizing your taxes. She finds possible credits and deductions for you, recommends tax-wise investments, and offers guidance on reducing your tax burden. She wants to protect as much of your hard-earned money as possible.

How Molly Examines Your Bank Information

Molly's advanced data analysis skills enable her to offer individualized financial guidance. Molly can produce valuable insights by analyzing large volumes of economic data with sophisticated algorithms and machine learning. This is how Molly examines your financial information:

1. Information Gathering

Molly gathers information from several sources, such as financial records, credit cards, investment accounts, and bank accounts. This information includes transaction history, account balances, earnings, outlays, and economic objectives. Your consent is obtained for all data collection, which is encrypted and stored securely.

2. Identification of Imprints

Molly analyzes your financial behaviour and finds patterns using machine learning algorithms. She examines your income trends, savings patterns, and spending habits to determine your financial profile. She can tell, for instance, if you tend to splurge during particular times of the year or if your income varies with the seasons.

3. Analysis of Predictive Data

Molly forecasts your future financial behaviour and results using predictive analysis. By looking at past data, she can predict future costs, possible savings, and investment returns. This enables her to give you proactive guidance and support you in making wise financial decisions.

4. Evaluation of Risk

Molly evaluates the risks involved in various financial choices, assessing the possible risks and profits. For instance, if you are thinking about making an investment, she will take into account your risk tolerance and market trends. This aids in your ability to make wise and well-rounded investing decisions.

5. Aligning Goals

Molly ensures that all financial guidance is in line with your long-term objectives. She monitors your progress toward your objectives and modifies her suggestions as necessary. Molly offers specialized guidance to help you reach your goals, whether you are saving for a down payment on a home, making retirement plans, or wanting to vacation.

6. Analysis of Behavior

Molly considers your spending patterns and behaviour. She is aware that behaviour and emotions have a role in financial decisions and that they are not always rational. Molly can offer guidance based on your behaviour that is not only financially sound but also reasonable and attainable by examining your spending and saving patterns.

7. Ongoing Education

Molly is an AI-powered coach who constantly learns from your behaviour and financial information. The more you engage with her, the better she understands your tastes and needs. Because of her ongoing education, Molly can hone her counsel and provide more precise and unique recommendations.

Actual Situations: How Molly Assists

To demonstrate how Molly can revolutionize money management, let us examine a few situations where Molly's tailored guidance has a significant influence.

Creating an Emergency Fund in Scenario 1

Thirty-year-old John is a working man who wishes to save emergency savings. Despite his stable income, he frequently needs help saving money.

Molly analyzes John's income and expenses, identifies discretionary spending areas, and offers a realistic savings plan. She advocates setting up automatic transfers to a high-yield savings account and provides ideas on eliminating unnecessary expenses. Over time, John successfully creates a large emergency fund, providing him with financial security.

Scenario 2: Reducing Credit Card Debt

Sarah has difficulty making many credit card payments because she has a lot of debt. Molly offers assistance. She examines Sarah's credit history, interest rates, and debt. Molly advises combining debts with high interest rates into one loan with a reduced interest rate. She also devises a payback schedule that puts the debt with the highest interest rate at the top. Molly also offers advice on creating a budget and cutting costs to help you have more money to pay off debt. According to Molly's advice, Sarah has better financial health and lowered her debt.

Scenario 3: Retirement Planning

A married couple in their 40s, Michael and Emily, are worried about their retirement funds. They want to ensure they can continue living the way they do after they retire. Molly examines their financial portfolio, anticipated retirement costs, and current funds. In addition to offering individualized retirement savings goals, she advises them to optimize their investing plan by combining low-risk and high-return investments. In addition, Molly provides advice on tax-efficient investments and suggests modifying contributions to utilize employer matching programs fully. With Molly's continued support, Michael and Emily feel confident and ready for retirement.

Scenario 4: Investment Optimization

Despite having a diversified portfolio, Linda is still determining if she is optimizing her returns as an investor. Considering Linda's risk tolerance and market movements, Molly examines her portfolio. She finds assets that could be performing better and recommends moving money to industries with better development prospects. Molly also offers advice on reducing tax obligations on investment gains and insights into new investment options. Linda improves her portfolio performance and returns with Molly's tailored guidance.

Managing Monthly Budget in Scenario Five

Tom recently graduated from college and is adjusting to his first job and autonomous money management. He needs help keeping track of his spending and frequently goes over budget. Molly assists Tom by examining his spending habits and compiling a thorough budget. She organizes his spending, places spending caps on discretionary categories, and sends him reminders in real-time when he is getting close to his spending cap. Molly advises him to keep an eye on his funds by utilizing tools and applications for budgeting. Tom develops sound financial habits and regains control over his expenditures under Molly's tutelage.

Molly is the AI-powered financial coach that is completely changing how people handle their money. Molly offers customized guidance that assists you in reaching your financial objectives through real-time data analysis, continuous learning, and personalized financial insights. Molly is your go-to advisor at every turn, helping you with emergency fund building, debt reduction, retirement planning, investment optimization, and monthly budget management.

Molly uses sophisticated algorithms and machine intelligence to provide relevant, doable, and financially aligned insights and recommendations. Because of her capacity to evaluate enormous volumes of financial data and spot patterns, you will get the most precise and customized advice possible.

Molly makes financial decisions more straightforward and empowers you to take charge of your financial destiny in a world where these decisions may be daunting and complicated. Join Molly in embracing AI's potential and enjoying the assurance and tranquility of wise financial choices.

Chapter 7: Success Stories and Testimonials from Users

Actual User Narratives

Speaking with people about their experiences is a great way to learn about money management solutions. Many people have benefited from Borrowell's assistance in achieving their goals and improving their financial situation. Here, we provide user stories to show how Borrowell has affected their lives.

First User Experience: Emily's Path to Financial Self-Sufficiency

The 28-year-old marketing specialist Emily has never been good at handling her money. She lived paycheck to paycheck and could not save money for the future, even though her income was respectable. Emily decided to take charge of her financial condition after learning about Borrowell.

"I was constantly worried about money before I started using Borrowell. My spending habits were uncontrollable, and I did not clearly understand my financial situation. I could assess my financial situation using Borrowell's complimentary credit report and score. The tailored suggestions were revolutionary. I used their recommended tools to create a budget and consolidate my credit card debt. I cleared off my credit card debt and began saving for a down payment on a house within a year. I gained the self-assurance and financial literacy I required from Borrowell." [Within a year, I was able to clear off my credit card debt and start saving for a house, which was a significant improvement from my previous financial situation].

User Experience 2: John's Road to Buying a House

John, a 35-year-old IT professional, had long desired home ownership but needed to be more comfortable with the mortgage application procedure. He went to Borrowell for advice, and the tailored suggestions were priceless.

"As I have always rented, owning a house intimidated me. My financial condition informed Borrowell's mortgage recommendations, which enabled me to locate a lender offering competitive terms. It made a difference with the thorough analysis of my credit record and advice on how to raise my score. I raised my credit score in less than two years and got a low-interest mortgage. I am happy to be a homeowner now because of Borrowell."

User Experience 3: Sarah's Path to Financial Freedom

Sarah, a 42-year-old nurse, battled to pay off her credit card debt and education debts. Borrowell's resources and tools enabled her to create a debt-free plan.

"It seemed like my debt would never go away. I needed to figure out how to approach it or where to begin. Borrowell's debt management tools gave me a detailed plan and doable actions to lower my debt. The tailored advice on combining my debts and getting cheaper interest rates was quite beneficial. With Borrowell's help, I made significant progress on my student loans and paid off my credit card debt. I am enthusiastic about the future and have more control over my finances.

Attainments

User success stories on Borrowell demonstrate the platform's natural advantages. These testimonies show how Borrowell has assisted people in reaching their financial goals and enhancing their general economic well-being.

Triumph Story 1: Mark's Investment Reach

Mark, a fifty-year-old engineer, has never invested with great caution. Borrowell's investment advice helped him make well-informed decisions that yielded substantial returns.

I was apprehensive about investing because I did not know much about it. For me, Borrowell's customized investment advice changed everything. Given my financial objectives and risk tolerance, they recommended a diversified portfolio. My investments have increased significantly over the last five years, and I am optimistic about my retirement funds. I felt more confident about making prudent investments and reaching my financial objectives thanks to Borrowell's advice."

Triumph Story 2: Lisa's Reversal of Finances

A thirty-year-old educator, Lisa had financial challenges due to unforeseen health-related costs. Borrowell improved her financial situation through individualized guidance and budgeting tools.

"I had financial hardships due to medical expenses, and I found it difficult to make ends meet." Using Borrowell's budgeting tools, I kept track of my spending and found places to make savings. Following their advice to work out a payback schedule and bargain with medical providers was really beneficial. I paid off my medical debts and saved an emergency fund in less than a year. The assistance I received from Borrowell was crucial in stabilizing my finances and taking back control."

Triumph Story 3: The Raising of James' Credit Score

James, a new graduate who was 25 years old, had considerable credit card debt and late payments, which negatively impacted his credit score. Borrowell was able to make things better thanks to his credit enhancement advice.

"Because of my poor credit score, I could not rent an apartment or obtain a car loan. The comprehensive credit report and tailored advice from Borrowell were just what I needed. I took their suggestion to pay off big bills and set up automatic payments. My credit score increased by more than 100 points last year. I successfully obtained a better apartment and a car loan with a competitive interest rate. I would not have been able to accomplish my goals and enhance my credit without Borrowell's advice."

How Borrowell Contributed to Better Financial Well-Being

Users have benefited from Borrowell's extensive toolkit in several ways, including improved financial health. Here, we examine a few crucial areas in which Borrowell has had a noteworthy influence.

1. Raising Credit Scores

Borrowell offers a free credit report and score for people who want to learn more about and take control of their credit. By providing comprehensive insights into their credit profiles, Borrowell assists consumers in identifying areas for improvement and taking proactive measures to raise their credit ratings. Numerous consumers have benefited from personalized advice that has raised credit scores and opened doors to more significant financial prospects. Examples of this advice include:

- Setting up automated payments.
- Lowering high credit card balances.
- Challenging errors on credit reports.

2. Handling debt

Although debt can be a heavy burden, Borrowell's debt management solutions give consumers the direction they need to deal with it successfully.

Users have reduced their debt more effectively because of Borrowell's individualized recommendations for debt consolidation, negotiating lower interest rates, and arranging payback schedules. By heeding Borrowell's guidance, users have improved their financial stability and decreased stress by paying off credit card debt, student loans, and other liabilities.

3. Expense management and budgeting

Borrowell's budgeting tools assist customers in creating and adhering to budgets that fit their goals and lifestyles. Effective budgeting is essential for financial wellness. Borrowell offers insights into discretionary spending and analyzes spending trends to assist consumers in finding areas where they may make savings and reduce expenditures. With the help of Borrowell's budgeting tools, consumers can better control their costs, prevent overspending, and develop sound financial practices.

4. Investment and Savings Techniques

Borrowell's tailored investing and savings recommendations help users accumulate money and meet their long-term financial objectives. Borrowell makes personalized recommendations for investing possibilities and saving techniques based on users' financial profiles and aspirations, considering their risk tolerance. Borrowell's advice has assisted clients in growing their assets and savings, regardless of whether they are saving for retirement, a significant purchase, or an emergency fund. This has enhanced their financial security and future prospects.

5. Advice on Mortgages and Homeownership

Borrowell's mortgage advice and recommendations have benefited people trying to purchase a property and navigate the challenging mortgage procedure. Borrowell has assisted customers in obtaining favourable mortgage terms and realizing their aspirations of becoming homeowners by offering customized mortgage choices depending on their financial circumstances and credit histories. Borrowell's advice on raising credit ratings and putting money down for a down payment has helped customers accomplish their dream of becoming homeowners.

6. Insurance Guide Advice

With Borrowell's specialized insurance suggestions, users can select the ideal coverage for their needs and be confident they are sufficiently safeguarded against any threats. By examining consumers' financial profiles and insurance requirements, Borrowell recommends insurance plans that provide the best coverage and benefits. Whether consumers search for life, house, vehicle, or health insurance, Borrowell's advice has enabled them to make well-informed choices and obtain the necessary security.

7. Empowerment and Education in Finance

In addition to offering suggestions and tools, Borrowell empowers consumers with financial literacy. Borrowell assists consumers in increasing their financial literacy and making wise decisions by providing resources, articles, and advice on a range of financial subjects. Users are now more equipped to take charge of their financial destinies because of the increased financial confidence and literacy brought about by this empowerment.

The effects of Borrowell on its users' financial well-being are extensive and significant. With tailored advice, all-inclusive resources, and insightful analysis, Borrowell has assisted people in raising their credit scores, controlling debt, creating sensible budgets, saving and investing sensibly, and reaching significant financial goals like becoming homeowners. Real user testimonials and success stories illustrate the advantages of utilizing Borrowell, showing how the platform has changed people's lives and enabled them to reach their financial objectives.

Through cutting-edge technology and data analytics, Borrowell gives consumers the direction and assistance they require to negotiate the challenges of financial management successfully. Borrowell is a reliable partner in assisting users in achieving economic success and well-being, regardless of whether they are just beginning their financial adventures or looking to optimize their current strategy.

The platform's beneficial effects will increase as more people utilize Borrowell for financial advice, assisting even more users in realizing their financial goals and safeguarding their futures. Everyone can achieve prosperity and economic freedom with Borrowell's help.

Chapter 8: Use QR Codes and Links

Convenience and empowerment go hand in hand in the digital age. Recognizing this, Borrowell has integrated QR codes and referral links into its platform, empowering users to manage their finances and expedite access to various services. With these tools, customers can instantly access Borrowell's offers, get personalized recommendations, and utilize the platform's capabilities more easily than ever before.

Simplifying the User Interface

1. Simplified Navigation

Utilizing QR codes and referral links makes navigating Borrowell's wide range of services more accessible. Users no longer have to go through the frequently tiresome process of looking for particular features or tools. Whether they are checking their credit score, asking for a personal loan, or accessing educational materials, customers can get to the desired service with just one scan of a QR code or click on a referring link.

2. Immediate Access to Customized Resources

Referral links and QR codes allow users to access need-specific financial resources efficiently. A QR code on Borrowell's promotional materials, for instance, can swiftly take users to a credit score checker or a personalized loan calculator. This immediacy ensures that customers can make well-informed financial decisions while enhancing their user experience.

3. Smooth Platform-to-Platform Integration

Borrowell has created refer links and QR codes that seamlessly function on various devices, including desktops, tablets, and mobile phones. This cross-platform interoperability ensures that Borrowell's services are always at users' fingertips, offering a truly flexible and connected financial management experience.

4. Strengthened Defense

Borrowell offers users a safe way to access its services using QR codes and referral links. The encryption and uniqueness of each QR code guarantee the privacy and security of user data. Thanks to this security feature, users may rest easy knowing that their financial information is protected and handled with the utmost care.

5. Effective Customer Service

Moreover, QR codes and referral links expedite customer assistance services. A quick scan or click can route users with problems or who need help to particular support sites or chat services. By allowing direct access, users can get help more quickly and effectively while also spending less time exploring menus.

How to Scan Barcodes

In today's tech-driven world, QR codes, known as Quick Response codes, are commonplace. They provide a quick, simple, and safe method of accessing internet services and content. Borrowell has embraced this technology to improve user interaction and expedite access to its financial tools and services. Here's how customers can take full advantage of Borrowell's offers using QR codes:

1. Using the Camera on a Smartphone to Scan QR Codes

The majority of contemporary smartphones include built-in QR code scanning functionality. To utilize the QR code, users only need to launch their camera app, align it with the code, and press the resulting notification. They will not require further apps because this will take them to the associated Borrowell service or resource.

Utilizing an App to Scan QR Codes

Many free QR code scanner apps are available in app stores for people whose smartphones cannot read QR codes. After downloading and opening the app, users can access the appropriate Borrowell service by scanning the QR code.

2. Receiving the Credit Score and Report from Borrowell Services

Users can obtain their credit report and score immediately by scanning a QR code connected to Borrowell's credit score service. This offers quick information about the state of their credit and tailored advice on strengthening it.

Applications for Personal Loans

Personal loan applications with QR codes expedite the procedure. Users can begin the loan application process immediately by scanning the form rather than going through several pages.

Teaching Materials

QR codes allow users to access articles, seminars, and videos from Borrowell quickly. This increases accessibility to financial education and lets people learn more whenever it is convenient for them.

3. Improving Budgeting Tools for Financial Health

QR codes can link to Borrowell's budgeting tools, allowing users to quickly access features that assist in tracking spending, setting financial goals, and managing budgets efficiently.

Solutions for Debt Management

QR codes can give consumers with financial difficulties instant access to Borrowell's debt management tools. This includes techniques for debt consolidation, advice on lowering interest rates, and individualized programs for repaying debt.

Financial Guidance

Users who scan QR codes connected to Borrowell's investing advisory services can receive personalized suggestions depending on their risk tolerance and financial objectives. Instant access to investment tools facilitates speedy and informed decision-making for users.

4. Special Offers

Special Savings

Borrowell users frequently receive special discounts and incentives. Promo materials with QR codes can link consumers to these deals, preventing them from missing out on important cost savings.

Bonuses for referrals

Users can rapidly refer friends and relatives to Borrowell's platform by scanning QR codes connected to the referral program. This offers customers referral bonuses and contributes to the expansion of Borrowell's community.

5. Security Points to Remember

Making Certain Authenticity

Users should only scan codes from reliable sources to guarantee their security and legitimacy. Borrowell's QR codes can only be obtained via its official platforms, which include its website, mobile app, and approved marketing materials.

Safeguarding Individual Data

Protecting personal information is essential for users who use QR codes to access financial services. Borrowell gives consumers peace of mind by ensuring that all data sent via QR codes is secure and encrypted.

Referral Program Advantages

Borrowell's referral program aims to compensate users for introducing others to the site. This program creates a win-win scenario for the referred person and the referrer. Here's a thorough analysis of the advantages of Borrowell's referral scheme.

1. Receive Financial Incentives for Referrals

One of the main advantages of Borrowell's referral program is the ability to earn money. For each successful referral, the referrer may receive a cash bonus or a credit toward Borrowell's premium services. Users now have a concrete motivation to tell others about their wonderful experiences.

Vouchers & Gift Cards

Borrowell offers prominent merchants gift cards, vouchers, and cash benefits as referral incentives. This increases the referral program's excitement and diversity, making users more attractive.

2. Facilitating Family and Friends' Access to Financial Resources

Users who recommend friends and family to Borrowell assist their loved ones in gaining access to strong financial resources and tools. This can significantly improve their financial situation by giving them the information and assistance they need to handle their money wisely.

Better Financial Situation

Making a referral to Borrowell can assist someone in achieving their financial objectives, managing debt, and raising their credit score. It can be immensely satisfying for the referrer to know that they have helped a loved one succeed financially.

3. Establishing a Community of Finance

Growing the Number of Users

Each recommendation contributes to expanding Borrowell's user base and forming a wider group of wise financial people. With a more extensive user base, the platform can offer more individualized recommendations and develop its offerings.

Comparable Experiences

A wider community results in more success stories and shared experiences. Users can benefit from one another's experiences, advice, and tactics, fostering a cooperative environment that is advantageous to all parties.

4. Early Entry and Exclusive Access to New Features

Borrowell frequently gives referrers early access to new features and tools as a thank-you. This helps consumers remain ahead of the curve by providing them with an early look at the latest additions and advancements to the platform.

Opportunities for Beta Testing

It is possible to invite referrers to participate in beta testing of upcoming features. This will provide them with an early look at new tools and enable them to offer insightful comments that will help mold Borrowell's future product offerings.

5. Enhanced Incentives for Retention and Engagement Over Time

In order to keep customers interested and inspired to recommend others, Borrowell's referral program offers continuous rewards. Seasonal promotions, unique benefits, and frequent reward updates make sure the program stays engaging and profitable over time.

Increased Customer Loyalty

Borrowell's referral program improves customer retention by offering material rewards and acknowledging user loyalty. Users happy with the platform are more inclined to stick around and tell others about their great experiences, which feeds the platform's growth and engagement cycle.

6. User-Friendly Interface with Simplified Referral Process

Borrowell has made it simple and quick to utilize its referral program. It is easy to share with others because users can access their QR codes and special referral links straight from the app or website.

Monitor the Status of Referrals

Users get real-time access to track their referral progress, including the number of successful recommendations and the prizes they have received. Because of this openness, users can remain motivated to recommend new people because they are always aware of their referral status.

Borrowell's use of QR codes and referral links, together with an extensive referral scheme, is an example of the platform's dedication to improving user experience and creating a helpful financial community. Borrowell allows consumers to take charge of their financial health and spread the word about their excellent experiences by offering expedited access to services, individualized financial tools, and lucrative referral bonuses.

Whether you apply for a personal loan with a referring link, check your credit score with a QR code, or join the referral network to receive benefits, Borrowell's cutting-edge features make money management more accessible, effective, and enjoyable. With Borrowell, embrace the power of community and technology to help you reach your financial objectives.

Chapter 9: Opening to Borrowell Registration

The Borrowell registration procedure is simple, fast, and user-friendly. It offers a smooth onboarding experience whether you want to manage debt, monitor your credit score, or investigate financial solutions.

The Easy Way to Sign Up

1. Go to the Borrowell Website

To begin the registration process, go to the Borrowell website. Scanning the QR code below will allow you to access the website on your computer or mobile device.

2. Register for an Account

Find the "Sign Up" button on the webpage after you have arrived. It is often in the upper right corner. To begin the registration procedure, click on it.

3. Provide your contact details.

You will be required to enter basic personal information like your name, email address, and birthdate. This information is required to establish your Borrowell account and confirm your identification.

4. Confirm Your Email Address

After you submit your personal data, Borrowell will email a verification email to your specified address. To verify your email address, check your inbox and click the verification link. You must take this action to guarantee the security of your account.

5. Create a Strong Password

Next, create a strong, secure password for your account. Borrowell might offer instructions on how to make a password that combines capital and lowercase letters, digits, and special characters. This improves your account's security.

6. Finish Up Your Profile

You will be prompted to finish your profile after your email has been validated and your password has been set. This could also contain further data like your address, job description, and financial facts. Completing your profile facilitates the provision of tailored financial recommendations from Borrowell.

7. Accept the conditions as stated.

Before completing your account, you must read and accept Borrowell's terms and conditions. These cover Borrowell's authorization to use your information for financial services and privacy policy.

8. Go to Your Dashboard

Once you have completed all the processes, you will be able to access your Borrowell dashboard. Here, you may check your credit score, review financial products, and use Borrowell's information and tools.

Using the Platform

Borrowell's platform interface is simple and intuitive. The site is easy to use and navigate, whether you are a returning member or a first-time user. Here's a summary of the main attributes and how to utilize them.

1. Overview of the Dashboard

The dashboard is the focal point of your Borrowell account. You can use all of Borrowell's features and tools from this location. The dashboard usually has multiple areas, each emphasizing a distinct facet of your financial situation.

Summary of Credit Score

Your current credit score summary appears at the top of your dashboard. This comprises the number representing your credit score, your credit rating (such as excellent, good, or fair), and any recent changes to your score.

Particularized Suggestions

Below the credit score summary, you can discover recommendations for specific financial products. Credit cards, loans, and insurance products are among the customized financial solutions based on your credit profile and objectives.

Current Operations

The recent activity area gives you a quick overview of financial transactions, including new accounts, credit queries, and credit report modifications. This keeps you updated on any changes made to your financial profile.

Finance insights

Moreover, Borrowell provides financial advice based on your spending patterns and credit records. This section offers pointers and recommendations for lowering debt, managing credit, and conserving money.

2. Report and Credit Score

Letting individuals view their credit reports and score for free is one of Borrowell's main features. How to use this part is as follows:

Check Your Credit Rating

Select the "Credit Score" tab from the dashboard menu to access your detailed credit score. This page breaks down the various elements that make up your credit score, such as credit inquiries, credit use, and payment history.

Get Your Credit Report Here

You can download a copy of your whole credit report from the exact location. This report contains comprehensive details about your credit accounts, payment history, and any credit-related infractions.

Simulator for Credit Score

Borrower's credit score simulator tool helps you evaluate how various financial decisions could affect your credit score. For example, you can mimic the results of closing a credit card debt or starting a new loan account.

3. Monetary Goods

Borrowell offers tailored advice on various financial goods, such as loans, credit cards, and insurance. How to investigate and apply for these products is as follows:

Credit Cards To receive customized credit card recommendations, click the "Credit Cards" page. Every card listing contains information about the card's attributes, perks, and prerequisites. Through the Borrowell portal, you can apply directly and compare several cards.

Loans There are recommendations for personal loans, debt consolidation loans, and other loans under the "Loans" area. Borrowell offers details on loan terms, interest rates, and qualifying requirements. This section lets you apply immediately for a loan that meets your needs.

Protection

Recommendations for several kinds of insurance, such as life, home, and auto insurance, are available under the "Insurance" category. To assist you in locating the most excellent coverage at the most affordable price, Borrowell examines several insurance companies and policies.

4. Tools for Budgeting

A sound budget is essential to financial stability. Borrowell provides you with several options to assist in budget management:

Expense Monitoring

Using the cost tracker lets you keep tabs on and organize your spending. You may track your progress and establish monthly spending limitations for several categories (such as food and entertainment).

Planner of Budgets

With the aid of the budget planner, you can make a thorough monthly budget. To obtain an overview of your financial condition, enter your income, fixed expenses (such as rent and utilities), and variable spending (like eating out and shopping).

Savings Objectives

Borrowell's savings goals feature helps you set and monitor savings goals. This application helps you stay motivated and on track when saving money for a big purchase, a vacation, or an emergency fund.

5. Handling debt

A vital component of sound financial management is debt management. Borrowell offers materials and strategies to assist you in successfully managing your debt:

Calculator for Debt Repayment

The debt payback calculator allows you to enter your monthly payments, interest rates, and loan sums. It then offers a thorough repayment schedule that includes the total amount of interest paid and the amount of time needed to pay off your loan.

Choices for Debt Consolidation

Borrowell provides advice for debt consolidation loans that may result in reduced interest rates and a more straightforward repayment schedule. This segment offers details on several loan alternatives and the application process.

Credit Guidance

Borrowell offers credit counselling programs to customers with high debt. These services provide individualized guidance and assistance to help customers create a plan for paying off debt and strengthening their financial situation.

6. Educational Materials

A fundamental component of Borrowell's purpose is financial education. To assist users in becoming more financially literate, the site provides a multitude of instructional resources:

Guides and Articles

Borrowell's blog offers tutorials and articles on a range of money-related subjects, such as investing, budgeting, and credit management. These resources offer insightful analysis and useful advice on money management.

Sessions Online and Offline

Borrowell offers workshops and webinars on a variety of financial subjects. During these live sessions, you can ask questions, gain deeper insights into particular areas of interest, and learn from financial professionals.

Financial Terminology

The financial vocabulary is an extensive resource that clarifies important financial phrases and concepts. Users unfamiliar with industry language and new to financial management will find this tool especially helpful.

Advice to Make the Most of Your Borrowell Experience

Making the most of Borrowell requires efficiently using the tools and resources available on the platform. To make the most of your time at Borrowell, consider the following advice:

1. Verify Your Credit Score Frequently

You must routinely check your credit score to keep your credit in good shape. To keep up with any changes to your credit score and report, visit your

Borrowell dashboard once a month or more. This will assist you in quickly identifying any errors or fraudulent activity.

2. Adhere to Specific Guidelines

Based on your financial objectives and credit profile, Borrowell makes tailored suggestions for financial products. Use these suggestions to locate loans, credit cards, and insurance that meet your needs. You may enhance your financial well-being and make wise decisions with tailored counsel.

3. Make Use of Budgeting Resources

Financial success is mainly dependent on effective budgeting. With Borrowell's budgeting tools, you can make a realistic budget, monitor your spending, and establish savings targets. You can stay on track by updating your budget regularly, monitoring your expenditures and preventing overspending.

4. Make Use of Debt Management Tools

Borrowell's debt management resources can assist you in creating a repayment plan if you are in debt. Make a thorough plan using the debt payback calculator, and look into debt consolidation options to lower interest rates and streamline payments.

5. Utilize Learning Resources

Borrowell offers a multitude of educational tools, such as webinars, workshops, and publications. To improve your financial literacy, make the time to read articles, watch webinars, and take part in workshops. Gaining a deeper comprehension of financial topics will enable you to make more informed decisions.

6. Configure Notifications and Alerts

You may set up alerts and notifications with Borrowell for various financial activities, such as nearing spending restrictions, new credit inquiries, and changes to your credit score. Turn on these alerts to remain informed and act quickly as necessary.

7. Mention Family and Friends

Utilize Borrowell's referral program to help friends and family become better financially literate while earning rewards. Sharing Borrowell helps others, and it also earns you bonuses for referring people.

8. Maintain an Up-to-Date Profile

Ensure the information on your Borrowell profile is always accurate and up to date. This includes your financial information, employment status, and contact details. Borrowell needs an accurate profile to give the most pertinent and individualized recommendations.

9. Carefully Examine Financial Product Offers

Examine financial product offers and review the terms and conditions. Ensure you know the interest rates, costs, and eligibility requirements before applying for a credit card, loan, or insurance policy. Making well-informed judgments will enable you to choose the best items for your needs and prevent needless expenses.

10. When in doubt, get professional counsel

Even while Borrowell offers a wealth of tools and services, there can be occasions when you require individualized financial guidance. Always be bold and ask for assistance from a credit counsellor or financial advisor, particularly if you are struggling with severe debt or complicated financial problems.

Starting a Borrowell account is a thrilling first step toward regaining control over your financial situation. You may make well-informed decisions, enhance your credit score, and accomplish your financial objectives through registration, efficient platform navigation, and utilization of diverse tools and resources. To get the most out of your Borrowell experience, remember to monitor your credit score regularly, heed individualized advice, and utilize instructional materials. Borrowell can assist you in laying a solid financial foundation and securing a more promising economic future with commitment and aggressive management.

About the Author

Richardson Rolls' career in teaching, writing, and corporate collaboration has greatly impacted financial literacy and education. His journey began in a tiny town, where his parents, both teachers, instilled in him a love for learning. This upbringing, coupled with his academic achievements-a bachelor's degree in English literature and a master's degree in education—lays the foundation for his first book, "Narratives of Learning: Stories from the Classroom," and his best-selling book, "Financial Literacy for All: A Practical Guide," both written during his freelance writing days. These books, along with his work in curriculum building for Borrowell, stand as a testament to his expertise and thought leadership in the field.

Richardson's teaching philosophy strongly emphasizes the transformational process to foster collaboration between teachers and students. He has developed training materials for personal finance and conducted workshops and seminars on various educational topics. One of the leading financial technology companies, Borrowell, has profited from his work in curriculum building.

Richardson is not just a teacher, but a passionate advocate for financial literacy. He sees it as a cornerstone of individual freedom and societal well-being. His work with groups, talks, and workshops for nonprofits, educational institutions, and community organizations, coupled with his thought leadership in financial education, is truly inspiring. He shares his knowledge and encourages people to proactively approach financial education through various platforms, igniting a fire for financial literacy in all who listen.

In conclusion, Richardson Rolls' influence is not confined to the classroom or the written page. His significant impact on personal finance and education, coupled with his work with Borrowell, is a testament to his expertise. By shaping the company's training initiatives, he has empowered its clients and left an indelible mark on the corporate world, proving his prowess in the field of financial literacy and education.

www.ingramcontent.com/pod-product-compliance
Lightning Source LLC
Chambersburg PA
CBHW071917210526
45479CB00002B/457